VIEWPOINTS®
SERIES

I The United Nations

Other Books of Related Interest:

Opposing Viewpoints Series

Agricultural Subsidies

Globalization

The Middle East Peace Process

At Issue Series

AIDS in Developing Countries

Is There a New Cold War?

Should There Be an International Climate Treaty?

Current Controversies Series

Fair Trade

Human Trafficking

The World Economy

"Congress shall make
no law . . . abridging
the freedom of speech,
or of the press."

First Amendment to the U.S. Constitution

The basic foundation of our democracy is the First Amendment guarantee of freedom of expression. The Opposing Viewpoints Series is dedicated to the concept of this basic freedom and the idea that it is more important to practice it than to enshrine it.

The United Nations

Laura Egendorf, Book Editor

GREENHAVEN PRESS
A part of Gale, Cengage Learning

Detroit • New York • San Francisco • New Haven, Conn • Waterville, Maine • London

Christine Nasso, *Publisher*
Elizabeth Des Chenes, *Managing Editor*

For more information, contact:
Greenhaven Press
27500 Drake Rd.
Farmington Hills, MI 48331-3535
Or you can visit our Internet site at gale.cengage.com

Articles in Greenhaven Press anthologies are often edited for length to meet page requirements. In addition, original titles of these works are changed to clearly present the main thesis and to explicitly indicate the author's opinion. Every effort is made to ensure that Greenhaven Press accurately reflects the original intent of the authors. Every effort has been made to trace the owners of copyrighted material.

Cover Image copyright © Unweit|Dreamstime.com.

LIBRARY OF CONGRESS CATALOGING-IN-PUBLICATION DATA

The United Nations / Laura Egendorf, Book Editor.
    p. cm. -- (Opposing viewpoints)
    Includes bibliographical references and index.
    ISBN 978-0-7377-4841-3 (hardcover) -- ISBN 978-0-7377-4842-0 (pbk.)
    1. United Nations. 2. United Nations--United States. I. Egendorf, Laura K., 1973-
    JZ4984.5.U5355 2011
    341.23--dc22

                                                                2010030902

Printed in the United States of America
1 2 3 4 5 6 7 14 13 12 11 10

Contents

Chapter 3: Should the United States Support the United Nations?

Chapter 4: What Is the Future of the United Nations?

Why Consider Opposing Viewpoints?

> *"The only way in which a human being can make some approach to knowing the whole of a subject is by hearing what can be said about it by persons of every variety of opinion and studying all modes in which it can be looked at by every character of mind. No wise man ever acquired his wisdom in any mode but this."*
>
> *John Stuart Mill*

In our media-intensive culture it is not difficult to find differing opinions. Thousands of newspapers and magazines and dozens of radio and television talk shows resound with differing points of view. The difficulty lies in deciding which opinion to agree with and which "experts" seem the most credible. The more inundated we become with differing opinions and claims, the more essential it is to hone critical reading and thinking skills to evaluate these ideas. Opposing Viewpoints books address this problem directly by presenting stimulating debates that can be used to enhance and teach these skills. The varied opinions contained in each book examine many different aspects of a single issue. While examining these conveniently edited opposing views, readers can develop critical thinking skills such as the ability to compare and contrast authors' credibility, facts, argumentation styles, use of persuasive techniques, and other stylistic tools. In short, the Opposing Viewpoints Series is an ideal way to attain the higher-level thinking and reading skills so essential in a culture of diverse and contradictory opinions.

In addition to providing a tool for critical thinking, Opposing Viewpoints books challenge readers to question their own strongly held opinions and assumptions. Most people form their opinions on the basis of upbringing, peer pressure, and personal, cultural, or professional bias. By reading carefully balanced opposing views, readers must directly confront new ideas as well as the opinions of those with whom they disagree. This is not to argue simplistically that everyone who reads opposing views will—or should—change his or her opinion. Instead, the series enhances readers' understanding of their own views by encouraging confrontation with opposing ideas. Careful examination of others' views can lead to the readers' understanding of the logical inconsistencies in their own opinions, perspective on why they hold an opinion, and the consideration of the possibility that their opinion requires further evaluation.

Evaluating Other Opinions

To ensure that this type of examination occurs, Opposing Viewpoints books present all types of opinions. Prominent spokespeople on different sides of each issue as well as well-known professionals from many disciplines challenge the reader. An additional goal of the series is to provide a forum for other, less known, or even unpopular viewpoints. The opinion of an ordinary person who has had to make the decision to cut off life support from a terminally ill relative, for example, may be just as valuable and provide just as much insight as a medical ethicist's professional opinion. The editors have two additional purposes in including these less known views. One, the editors encourage readers to respect others' opinions—even when not enhanced by professional credibility. It is only by reading or listening to and objectively evaluating others' ideas that one can determine whether they are worthy of consideration. Two, the inclusion of such viewpoints encourages the important critical thinking skill of objectively evaluating an author's credentials and bias. This evaluation will illuminate an author's reasons for taking a particular stance on an issue and will aid in readers' evaluation of the author's ideas.

It is our hope that these books will give readers a deeper understanding of the issues debated and an appreciation of the complexity of even seemingly simple issues when good and honest people disagree. This awareness is particularly important in a democratic society such as ours in which people enter into public debate to determine the common good. Those with whom one disagrees should not be regarded as enemies but rather as people whose views deserve careful examination and may shed light on one's own.

Thomas Jefferson once said that "difference of opinion leads to inquiry, and inquiry to truth." Jefferson, a broadly educated man, argued that "if a nation expects to be ignorant and free . . . it expects what never was and never will be." As individuals and as a nation, it is imperative that we consider the opinions of others and examine them with skill and discernment. The Opposing Viewpoints Series is intended to help readers achieve this goal.

David L. Bender and Bruno Leone,
Founders

Introduction

> *"The continued push for economic, political and military dominance by the big powers of the North gives cause for concern that global governance institutions become even more the instruments for asserting such dominance."*
>
> —The South Centre,
> What UN for the 21st Century?
> A New North-South Divide.

> *"Using the North-South dichotomy to explain policy disagreements potentially blinds one to the nuances of very complex issues, making it more difficult for policymakers to develop effective strategies."*
>
> —Paul Romita,
> *"Deconstructing the
> North-South Label,"*
> International Peace Institute

With 192 members, finding consensus in the United Nations is virtually impossible, as nations form factions on the basis of religion, form of government, geography, and other commonalities. Perhaps the greatest split in the UN is the North-South divide. This term does not refer to nations in the Northern and Southern hemispheres, but rather to developed versus developing nations. The "North," which includes the United States, Japan, and the European Union, as well as other Western democracies, has historically held much of the power in the UN due its greater financial resources. However, as the nations of the South continue to grow in both population and influence, conflicts between the two sides have deepened. This division is especially evident in two worldwide issues that the UN is trying to tackle: global warming and control of the UN budget.

The United Nations has tried its hand at reducing global warming. In 1997, the organization adopted the Kyoto Protocol. Under the terms of the protocol, the thirty-seven industrialized nations were to reduce their greenhouse gas emissions. The problem with this agreement, its critics contend, is that southern nations with burgeoning populations are actually creating more greenhouse gases but are not expected to reduce their impact on the environment. Some analysts believe this North-South divide is unfair to developed nations. Greg Mastel, Stephen Kho, and Bernd Janzen write in the journal *International Economy* that no matter what steps the United States and other northern nations take, they cannot counteract the effects of developing nations. The authors argue: "China has become the world's leading emitter of greenhouse gases, and other developing countries are not far behind. Developed countries—notably the United States—are still major emitters, but even if the developed world took heroic measures to sharply reduce future emissions, those reductions would be completely swamped by continued increases in developing world emissions."

Still others argue that it is not fair to place the onus for reducing global warming on the South. In a piece she wrote for *CounterCurrents*, Helena Norberg-Hodge maintains that most of the manufacturing that takes place in the South is to create goods for the North. She argues that the South cannot be told how it should reduce its greenhouse gas emissions. Instead, writes Norberg-Hodge, the best path for southern nations to take to reduce emissions is "to strengthen the existing, decentralized demographic pattern by keeping villages and small towns alive. This would allow communities to maintain social cohesion and a closer contact with the land."

A second issue that brings the North-South divide at the UN to light is the organization's budget. Conflicts have arisen in the past between the United States, Japan, and the European Union—which, combined, pay for more than 80 percent of the UN's annual budget—and the rest of the organization. These northern nations want more say over how the UN is run, because financial support is almost entirely in their hands. However, they are vastly outnumbered by the southern nations, who can use their voting majority to thwart northern power plays. As UN deputy secretary-general Mark Malloch Brown explains, such acrimony is "not an issue of just management. This [is] about power and the future control of the organisation." As long as one side of the divide has the money and the other side has the votes, future tugs-of-war between the North and South are destined to persist.

For more than six decades, the United Nations has both brought nations together and placed them on opposite sides of a given issue. In *Opposing Viewpoints: The United Nations*, the contributors debate the successes and failures of the UN in the following chapters: Is the United Nations Effective? Is the United Nations Impartial Toward the Middle East? Should the United States Support the United Nations? What Is the Future of the United Nations? It is hoped that careful consideration of the viewpoints in this book will help the reader better understand the challenges facing the preeminent global organization.

Chapter 1

Is the United Nations Effective?

Chapter Preface

One of the major roles of the United Nations is to establish and oversee peacekeeping forces around the world. Typically located in war-torn or poverty-stricken nations, UN peacekeepers have one of the world's most dangerous jobs. Since 2003, more than nine hundred peacekeepers have died as a result of accidents, illnesses, or more violent means. For example, UN peacekeeping endured its greatest tragedy in January 2010. The massive earthquake that struck Haiti caused the UN peacekeeping headquarters in that nation to collapse, resulting in ninety-six fatalities.

However, few places have proven more deadly to UN peacekeepers than the Darfur region of Sudan. Civil war has raged in Darfur since 2003, with more than two hundred thousand dead since the fighting began. Peacekeepers are often victims of the violence. Twenty-seven peacekeepers have been killed by hostile actions since a peacekeeping force was established in Darfur in 2008. Among the deadliest attacks was an ambush by two hundred gunmen in July 2008 that left seven peacekeepers dead. Five peacekeepers were killed in two attacks in May and June 2010.

Some people have expressed concern that these peacekeeping forces are not prepared for situations such as Darfur. Writing for the *International Herald Tribune*, Salim Salim contends that the African Union/United Nations Hybrid operation in Darfur (UNAMID), the force assigned to the region, has not been given essential resources or support. Salim writes: "If the international community is serious about fulfilling its responsibility to protect civilians in Darfur, it can start by providing the basics that UNAMID urgently needs. Such support could have saved some . . . peacekeepers who died [in July 2008] gallantly trying to protect civilians."

While the danger of peacekeeping may be difficult to dispute, many people question whether the UN's various efforts to improve the quality of life around the world have been effective. The contributors to this chapter debate the effectiveness of the United Nations in meeting its obligations.

| *"We endeavour together to enhance the efficiency and effectiveness of our work."*

The United Nations Is Increasing Its Effectiveness

Asha-Rose Migiro

In the following viewpoint, taken from a talk to the Vienna conference on UN coherence, Asha-Rose Migiro argues that the United Nations is effective and can become more so if it ends inefficiencies, supports national development priorities, and harmonizes its business practices. Should the UN achieve these goals, she contends, it will be even more successful at supporting development goals and improving the lives of people around the world. Migiro is deputy secretary-general of the United Nations.

As you read, consider the following questions:

1. What has contributed to incoherent UN policies, in Migiro's view?

2. In the author's opinion, why is the formal establishment of the United Nations Development Assistance Framework important?

Asha-Rose Migiro, "Efficient, Effective, Coherent United Nations Can Make Real Difference in Lives of People it Serves, Says Deputy Secretary-General to Vienna Conference," un.org, March 4, 2008. Reprinted with the permission of the United Nations.

3. According to Migiro, what are the challenges that remain for the United Nations system?

We have converged here today to agree on ways we can work together for a stronger and more coherent United Nations system. It's not often that many of us get to talk about these matters face to face, and I would like to thank the United Nations Industrial Development Organization (UNIDO) very much for giving us this opportunity. Excellencies, we need to seize this opportunity and reflect with open minds on how we can keep moving forward, how we can make the United Nations system more efficient, effective and coherent. As we move ahead, I urge all of you to keep a focus on the ultimate objectives: a United Nations that makes a real difference in the lives of the people that it serves; a United Nations that provides meaningful support for national development priorities; and a United Nations that helps countries to attain the internationally agreed development goals, including the Millennium Development Goals.

We all recognise that the United Nations can and should be an indispensable force driving forward the discourse on human development, by building a global consensus to scale up the implementation of the Millennium Development Goals, by playing a leading role in promoting sustainable development, by responding rapidly to humanitarian disasters and by mobilising international action to address global challenges such as climate change.

At the same time, we have also seen how the United Nations work on development and the environment is often fragmented and weak. Inefficient and ineffective governance and unpredictable funding have too often contributed to incoherent policies, duplication and operational paralysis across the system. Excellencies, as we are too well aware, cooperation between organizations has been hindered by competition for funding, mission creep and outdated business practices.

The UN Must Work Together

We cannot and we are not standing idle in the face of these challenges. We must keep working together to reduce this fragmentation and increase our effectiveness, efficiency and coherence as a development partner for Governments.

This positive change has been guided by our Member States through their consensual decision on the Triennial Comprehensive Policy Review (TCPR). We look forward to further guidance through ongoing discussions of the High-Level Panel's report on system-wide coherence. It is an honour to have with us today the co-chairs of the General Assembly process, and I am eager to hear from them on how best we can advance this important agenda.

We have already before us some initial lessons learned from the first year of the eight "Delivering as One" pilots [a UN development assistance program]. So far, they have given us a lot to think about and to act on.

I would like to draw your attention first of all to the foundation for our work, the 2007 Triennial Comprehensive Policy Review [TCPR], which has given the United Nations system a significant mandate to become more coherent, efficient and effective. The TCPR recognizes the central role of the Resident Coordinators in improving the effectiveness of the United Nations system's response to national development priorities. It also emphasizes that the Resident Coordinators, supported by the United Nations country teams, should report to national authorities on progress made against the results agreed in the United Nations Development Assistance Framework. On both counts, the TCPR emphasizes that the Resident Coordinators should play a central role in ensuring that the United Nations activities are aligned and accountable to national development strategies. This is essential if we are to create more coherent United Nations country teams.

Recent UN Success Stories

- *Maintaining the ceasefire in Lebanon.*
  After the ceasefire was accepted in mid-August 2006, the United Nations quickly increased the number of peacekeepers in southern Lebanon, allowing the Israeli army to pull back and Lebanese army to deploy to the border for the first time in decades. No serious breach of the ceasefire has occurred since; the UN discovered dozens of arms caches while monitoring for arms shipments.

- *Bringing a warlord to justice and inspiring democracy in Liberia.*
  In 2006 the United Nations helped bring to justice Liberian warlord Charles Taylor, who helped ignite a civil war that killed almost 150,000 people. The UN subsequently assisted in holding free elections and inaugurating Africa's first democratically elected female president, Ellen Johnson-Sirleaf.

- *Aiding millions displaced by conflict in Darfur.*
  Despite attacks on humanitarian aid workers, the World Food Program fed over 6.1 million people [in 2006] in southern Sudan, Darfur and eastern Chad, and the UN provided water, shelter, health care, and other necessities, thereby reducing deaths among the internally displaced by two-thirds.

- *Educating women in Afghanistan.*
  The Joint Partnership on Adult Functional Literacy, an endeavor of the Government of Afghanistan and UN agencies, launched a literacy program [in 2006], which reached an estimated 160,000 Afghans, mostly women.

Tim Wirth, testimony before the U.S. House Committee on Foreign Affairs, February 13, 2007.

Formally Establishing a Framework

I also think it's important that the TCPR formally establishes the United Nations Development Assistance Framework as a key instrument for bringing the United Nations system together in a more coherent and effective way that is aligned with national development priorities. The TCPR also emphasises that, in pursuing coherence and effectiveness, the system should strive for inclusiveness, drawing on the important mandates and expertise of all UN agencies in supporting national priorities.

These mandates from the TCPR, as well as others, provide us with guidance from the Member States as we endeavour together to enhance the efficiency and effectiveness of our work. . . .

The timing of our meeting is also opportune, as we can now more concretely discuss the progress made towards strengthening United Nations coherence, as well as the challenges that remain, with the benefit of the stocktaking process reports that have reflected on the pilot experience thus far. From the feedback from the Governments and from the United Nations country teams, we can already look to a number of lessons learned.

Of primary importance, national ownership and leadership is an essential component of increased coherence. It's clear that we can only support national priorities by working together as one United Nations system, bringing together our respective capacities and expertise.

I am very pleased that by all accounts—from United Nations country teams, United Nations agencies and, most importantly, from Governments themselves—the pilot experience has indeed demonstrated a more significant alignment with national development plans.

I am also pleased to hear that the pilot experience has achieved important strides in encouraging and enabling the United Nations system to work together as one, with a positive change in attitude and a greater drive to work in partnerships for greater impact—a message that again, I hear from Governments and from the United Nations organisations themselves.

Reform Is Moving Too Slowly

At the same time, we also need to discuss how to continue addressing the challenges that we still face. We need to recognise that the slow pace of reform and change at Headquarters is hindering the pilots. We have to ensure that the global tools and processes are in place to support and strengthen a more efficient United Nations at the country level. There needs to be increased clarity on Resident Coordinator authority and mutual accountability within the United Nations country team.

While we will have the chance to delve further into these issues . . . , we should also use this opportunity to find ways to surmount the challenges we will face as we move forward and seek to demonstrate concrete results.

First, I wish to see everyone working together to ensure that we implement the "One Programme" in the eight pilot [countries], and we have to ensure that they show real results. We must also ensure that Governments remain engaged and in the lead as we address the remaining difficult issues— including transaction costs—that are critical to the broader discussions on United Nations efficiency and coherence.

Second, as a system we need to distill the lessons we are learning from the pilots, and apply them to other United Nations country teams—where it's appropriate and requested by Member States. This gives us an important opportunity to realise the United Nations Development Assistance Framework as a key instrument in bringing us together to apply our mandates and expertise to supporting national priorities.

Third, those of us at Headquarters need to take full responsibility for providing our colleagues at the country level with the support and flexibility they need as they respond to national requests to become more coherent and efficient. In particular, we need to harmonize our business practices more quickly and effectively.

Finally, I would like to highlight the essential role that the specialised agencies and the non-resident agencies play in the United Nations system's overall effort to achieve greater efficiency, effectiveness and coherence, by drawing on your important mandates and expertise to support national development priorities. I think the fact that we are meeting here at UNIDO's headquarters symbolizes the importance of their role.

The UN Still Faces Many Challenges

I am particularly pleased to hear that, through the pilots, agencies were able to promote their mandates within the framework of United Nations agency cooperation, and that technical and advisory roles in their respective substantive mandates were reconfirmed, accepted and strengthened. And I have also heard that the pilots have encouraged many United Nations organisations to introduce internal adjustments to adapt to the changes stemming from this process.

At the same time, we would be remiss not to acknowledge the challenges that remain for the United Nations system as a whole, and certainly for the specialised agencies—the significant time and staff requirements; the different business models that create an inherent disadvantage for funding and participation; different cycles for programme planning; and limited experience with programming tools such as the United Nations Development Assistance Framework (UNDAF), to mention a few.

As we move forward, I would like to see even greater inclusiveness and more progress in how specialized agencies adjust their planning and budgeting systems to support robustly the "Delivering as One" pilots and greater United Nations coherence at the country level. We need to have oneness in our own agency to support Delivering as One more effectively. All this we must do while keeping national development priorities permanently in mind.

It is my hope that ... this meeting will allow us to reflect on how we can move forward, together, to concretely resolve these remaining challenges before us. The expectations on us are high, but the stakes are even higher. We must not forget that our paramount challenge is to demonstrate that true coherence and effectiveness in the United Nations ultimately leads to greater impact in improving the lives of the people in the countries we serve. We owe them nothing less.

| "The U.N. is an utterly useless organization."

The United Nations Is Utterly Ineffective

Jamal Bittar

In the following viewpoint Jamal Bittar asserts that the United Nations has failed to protect human rights and has not taken the actions needed to save lives in Sudan, Iraq, and other nations. In his view, the UN has achieved nothing in the six decades it has existed and will continue to serve no purpose unless it is overhauled completely. Bittar is a professor of interdisciplinary studies at the University of Toledo in Ohio.

As you read, consider the following questions:

1. According to the author, how did the United Nations treat Muslim men in Sarajevo?

2. In Bittar's view, what are the two conclusions that can be drawn regarding the United Nations?

3. What is the only purpose of the UN, in the author's opinion?

I used to think the U.N., both in principle and in practice, was the closest thing we'd have to a world government, coming together to tackle the challenges faced by all humanity. Now I feel that the U.N. is an utterly useless organization when it comes to protecting human rights and enforcing security.

A Litany of Failures

As we speak thousands are murdered in the Darfur region of the Sudan, and what does the U.N. do? They send troops to a different part of the country. Clearly, they are more concerned about being seen to be doing something, than actually doing it. And as the bureaucrats shuffle their papers in New York, and peacekeepers patrol the peaceful areas, more people are dying horrifying deaths a few miles away.

The U.N. has done more outrageous things in the past, as when it herded Muslim men into Sarajevo, methodically disarmed them and then handed them over to Serb militiamen to be shot, or when it ordered its commanding officer in Rwanda not to seize the arms caches that were about to be used for the genocide, which saw more than a million Tutsis dead and many more disabled or displaced.

The U.N. failed to stop the illegal invasion of Iraq, which has resulted in the death of thousands of civilians, and made Iraq worse than what it was under Saddam Hussein. It has not taken any action against Israel's failure to adhere to the U.N. resolutions dating years back or its disproportionate use of force against the Palestinians and Lebanese in the name of "self defense," which is a crime under international law.

The U.N. charges people like Charles Taylor of Liberia, Radovan Karadzic of Bosnia and others, but fails to charge people like George W. Bush and all Israeli prime ministers who have committed war crimes against humanity.

Further, the U.N. has strenuously denied covering up an investigation into the sale of illicit arms by its officials to Congolese rebels. I mean it's one thing to be called useless: sitting around in the aftermath of the Asian tsunami holding press conferences while the Australian and U.S. navies were on site distributing aid; it's another thing to be selling weapons to murderous militiamen: that's in the worse than useless category.

No Real Achievements

Seeing its pathetic demise is even more sickening considering the number of people who still defend it as the holy grail of morality and international law. And for those who support it, what has the U.N. exactly achieved in the last sixty years? Achieved peace in Europe? Ask the people in Bosnia. Settled the problem in the Middle East? Ask the people in Gaza. Improved life for Africans? Ask the people in Darfur, or Rwanda, or anybody for that matter.

Not only does it slow down the process of passing resolutions and making decisions, but it is often used for reasons personal to the country rather than legitimate reasons. Moreover, it is highly unfair that only five countries hold the veto power. Originally, they were given the power as "winners" of WWII and as the most powerful countries that existed when the U.N. was created, but this has long since changed. In the past 50 years, many countries have climbed to the top of the world podium as economically or politically more influential, and if veto power is allowed, they should be considered for it as well.

Lastly, veto power gives even more power to the already powerful. Why do the most influential countries in the world already need more power? The U.N. is supposed to be a democratic and diplomatic organization, but keeping veto power around hinders the fulfilment of this ideology as it diminishes the voices of smaller countries.

It's good as an organization at drawing up idealistic conventions, but near-useless at getting them translated into political reality. This usually prompts one or another of two con-clusions: first, that the U.N. is powerless, second that it is hypocritical—or worse, both. Welcome to the U.N.'s thou-sandth summit, scheduled to beat all previous records on ad-mirable promises, declarations of noble ideals and evocations of a peaceful and just future for humanity. It has ballooned into an organization of members in such radically different stages of their development that the core values of the United Nations are imperiled.

A Continuing Failure

The U.N., like the League of Nations before it, has shown the futility of trying to achieve a commonality of purpose among nations who do not share a common political philosophy or experience. The only purpose the U.N. serves is to provide a podium and an illusion of legitimacy for some of the vilest regimes on the planet.

It's extraordinary how we keep ignoring the actual U.N. in favor of some theoretical one. Even though much of its bu-reaucrats engage in fraud, and are found running smuggling rackets or child prostitution rings, we still maintain that the U.N. embodies a lofty ideal. And that, of course, is the prob-lem. The automatic benefit of the doubt will, over time, de-stroy even the most robust institution.

The U.N. has proven itself a failure for its entire history and will continue to do so. It's a diseased, toothless and impo-tent organization. Pretending anything different is nothing more than wishful thinking.

What is more disturbing is the unwillingness of many commentators to admit as much—because denial hinders any possibility of change. The U.N. requires a complete overhaul in order to salvage any useful function it could possibly serve—and even then it will still be a sclerotic, top-heavy, in-efficient body.

> *"For many who care about the universality and impartiality of human rights ... watching the council's progress has been a deeply disappointing experience."*

The UN Human Rights Council Faces Challenges

Barbara Crossette

Barbara Crossette argues in the following viewpoint that the UN Human Rights Council has failed to address human rights violations in nations such as Tibet, India, and Zimbabwe. She contends that the council has not been as successful as it could be due to regionalism and its inability to balance the differing views of human rights held by Western democracies, which value democracy and civil rights above all, and the developing world, which focuses on the rights to food and shelter. Crossette is a journalist who specializes in foreign policy and international affairs and the UN correspondent for the Nation *magazine.*

Barbara Crossette, "A Disappointing Record: Will the New Human Rights Council Take Its Mandate Seriously?" *America*, vol. 199, December 1, 2008, pp. 23–27. Copyright © 2008 www.americamagazine.org. All rights reserved. Reproduced by permission of America Press. For subscription information, visit www.americamagazine.org.

As you read, consider the following questions:

1. In its September 2008 agenda, what was the only country the council named in advance to receive special attention, according to Crossette?

2. As explained by the author, how many seats do Western European and "other" nations have on the Human Rights Council?

3. What does Crossette believe would be the greatest achievement of the Human Rights Council?

When leaders of governments from around the world met in the fall of 2005 at a summit marking the 60th anniversary of the founding of the United Nations, they agreed to a move that had seemed all but impossible in the contentious process of institutional reform: they abolished the discredited U.N. Commission on Human Rights and called for a fresh start with the formation of a new body to be called the Human Rights Council.

Creating a New Council

That was step one. By mid-March 2006, the General Assembly had taken step two: it established the Human Rights Council after barely six months of negotiating. This achievement was due largely to the sharply focused effort of the General Assembly president, Jan Eliasson, a former Swedish foreign minister and ambassador to the United States, who was determined not to let the usual U.N. drift carry this bold proposal into oblivion.

The General Assembly resolution declared flatly "that all members of the council shall uphold the highest standards in the promotion and protection of human rights." The old 54-member commission had become a refuge of scoundrel governments that sought seats more to defend themselves from international criticism than to support human rights anywhere. It was a bundle of entrenched biases, with an agenda pockmarked by glaring omissions.

Eliasson had the strong backing of Secretary General Kofi Annan, who had called for the abolition of the old commission in a milestone report titled *In Larger Freedom*. Annan also had spoken in plain language about how the commission had lost its credibility, was threatening to tarnish the United Nations itself, and why its sins should not be repeated by a new body.

"We are now witnessing a new beginning for the promotion and protection of human rights," Eliasson said when the job was done. Quoting from the General Assembly resolution that created the council, he added, "The work of the council will be guided by the principles of universality, impartiality, objectivity, non-selectivity and constructive international dialogue and cooperation, with a view to enhancing the promotion and protection of all human rights."

The Council Has Been Disappointing

The Human Rights Council, which assembled formally for the first time in June 2006, now has more than two-and-a-half years of work by which its record can be judged. For many who care about the universality and impartiality of human rights in both government and nongovernmental organizations, watching the council's progress has been a deeply disappointing experience.

Skimming over the violent collapse of civil rights in Zimbabwe, and barely touching on the culpability of Sudan's government for the nearly 300,000 deaths in Darfur, the council focused more than half of its seven special sessions since 2006 on the Israeli occupation of Arab territories. True, Burma (now called Myanmar by its military rulers) did receive attention, with calls to expand the political space. There was also a special session on global food prices and shortages. But the council chose not to consider Tibet, for example, or the mounting toll of official violence against minorities in India. Both China and India are council members.

On the council's agenda for September 2008, only one country was named in advance for special attention: Israel. Moreover, the council is now dealing with the explosive issue of what topics will dominate a conference on racism, xenophobia [fear of foreigners] and other forms of intolerance to be held in Durban, South Africa, [in 2009].

The Durban Controversy

Several nations are threatening to boycott the Durban meeting. They fear a sustained assault on the industrialized, ex-colonial "global North" and another on Israel, as well as demands for reparations and special programs for people of African descent, whether or not they were affected by the Atlantic slave trade. By contrast, they fear no demands will be made on behalf of those caught up in widespread slavery and bonded labor in Asia or Africa, which continues.

[The] meeting in Durban was planned to review actions taken since the first U.N. international conference was held there in 2001 on issues of racism and intolerance. That gathering erupted into acrimonious exchanges when participants decided to revive the "Zionism is racism" language that had been rooted out of the United Nations a decade earlier. The United States walked out of that first Durban conference, as did Israel.

The next Durban conference will be a trial by fire for the new U.N. High Commissioner for Human Rights, Navanethem Pillay, a South African who, coincidentally, began her distinguished legal career in Durban as an advocate for political prisoners under apartheid. Her office will oversee the Durban meeting. . . . Although the Human Rights Council and the office of the high commissioner, both based in Geneva, are expected to work in tandem, they are separate entities; and already there has been friction. A Nigerian, Martin Ihoeghian Uhomoibhi, is now president of the Human Rights Council.

Reforms Fell Short

Both the promise and the potential of the Human Rights Council are linked to its composition and working methods, as is the disappointing record it is rapidly accumulating. In creating the new body, it was imperative to ensure that the structural flaws of the commission not reemerge in the council during the give-and-take of intergovernmental negotiations.

For greater efficiency and coherence, the governments committed to genuine change wanted the new Human Rights Council to be smaller than the old 54-member commission. They argued that countries should have to demonstrate a reasonable human rights reputation to be elected, as its mandate demands, and should be open to continuing scrutiny as council members. Voting for members should be taken out of the horse-trading arena of the Economic and Social Council. There governments lobby for support in elections to such bodies or to U.N. agency boards, whether or not they have the qualifications to hold whatever seat is being contested. In the past, countries had pressed their perceived right to have a turn at membership on the 60-year-old Commission on Human Rights, and regions saw nothing wrong with awarding known offenders the commission's chairmanship when they had the chance.

Negotiations on the shape of the Human Rights Council were intense. When they concluded in spring 2006, there were losses and gains. The new council, which holds longer and more frequent sessions than the commission, has 47 members—not much smaller than its predecessor. But members were to be elected competitively by winning an absolute majority in secret balloting in the General Assembly, not by backroom deals within geographical regions. Africa was given

13 seats, Asia (which includes the Middle East) also 13, Eastern Europe (including Russia) 6, Latin America and the Caribbean 8, and Western Europe and "other" (sweeping in North America, New Zealand and Australia) 7.

Democracies Have Failed

The United States, whose delegation in negotiations was led by John Bolton, the ambassador to the United Nations in 2005–6 and a severe critic of both the organization and its principles, played a sorry role in these crucial talks. In keeping with his spoiler record at the United Nations, where he nearly sabotaged the 2005 summit agreement on a range of topics, Bolton raised numerous objections to Human Rights Council blueprints and forced compromises, only to walk away at the last minute, voting against the council and saying that Washington would not seek a seat.

While Americans have continued to be observers, the United States lost all rights and opportunities to shape the new body from inside. Friends of the United States are urging a new American leadership with a clean, or empty, slate on human rights, to reverse the Bolton decision and run for a council seat in 2009. Except for one hiatus in almost six decades, the United States had always been a member of the Commission on Human Rights.

Louise Arbour, a Canadian judge who was high commissioner for human rights from 2004 to 2008, reflected in an interview on what caused familiar problems to resurface in the Human Rights Council, and on how democratic nations failed to avert trouble before it became entrenched. She said that as high commissioner she had urged the new council in 2006 to move beyond the rigid emphasis on regional solidarity that in the past had blocked criticisms of offending governments and allowed them to serve on the commission. She advocated a much more universal or thematic approach, dealing with human rights violations in any given category wherever they occur.

Arbour also said that she had asked international blocs of like-minded countries—coalitions of democracies, the French-speaking countries and others—to promote global themes. Yet the only group that followed her advice, however inadvertently, was the Organization of the Islamic Conference. Their fixation on Israel, she said, has become the council's most consistent motivating theme. It did not have to be that way, she added.

Tackling Regionalism and Rights

Regionalism dies hard. It continues to affect voting for council members. In the June 2008 elections, for example, Africa nominated only four nations for four available African places on the council, a third of whose members are elected each year to prevent a total turnover. While the countries nominated still needed to win a majority of General Assembly votes, there was effectively no slate of Africans to choose from. Latin America also put forth only three nominees for three available seats. Other regions had more nominees than allotted seats. In the case of Africa, a consortium of human rights organizations that pooled existing international surveys of human and civil rights and freedom of expression categorized two of the four nations nominated (and ultimately elected) as "unqualified," one "questionable" and only one, Ghana, "qualified" to take a council seat.

For European, North American and other democracies as diverse as Japan, Botswana, Ghana, Brazil or Mexico, the council should provide an opportunity to demonstrate that there is a universal ethos in human rights that can transcend cultures, perhaps with a few adjustments. It should be imperative that governments seek to join an international conversation not blinkered by regional loyalties, and that thoughtful, even philosophical, minds are assigned to national delegations. Hisashi Owada, a legendary Japanese diplomat who is now a judge on the International Court of Justice in The Hague, spoke with great eloquence about universal values when he was Japanese ambassador to the United Nations in the 1990s. [South African president] Nelson Mandela's influence as a defender of rights and a conciliator of seemingly implacable foes was felt worldwide. Such people should set the standard.

In the process of bridging cultural gaps, Western human rights advocates may have to rethink some of their absolute insistence since the founding of the United Nations on the primacy of civil and political rights, Arbour said. Much of the developing world—the vast majority of humanity—wants to concentrate first or equally on survival. Persistent demands are made for more attention in U.N. human rights bodies for rights to food, shelter and other immediate needs. A functioning Human Rights Council would be the place for serious examination of how to balance the two approaches.

Among 29 "special raporteurs" the council oversees are those who issue tough, even accusatory or incendiary, reports on the rights to education or food, the rights of migrants, the roots of poverty and other issues that might seem more social than political. They document the importance of such issues and tend to find the rich nations culpable of letting down the rest. But it is also true that numerous governments in the developing world have avoided ensuring greater human rights and civil liberties by deflecting the discussion toward social and economic rights.

In some cases both civil and economic rights have been degraded. In Zimbabwe, for example, a high standard of living in the breadbasket of southern Africa was destroyed by Robert Mugabe, a dictator with the blood of political opponents on his hands. Amartya Sen, the Nobel Prize–winning economist, has argued that famines do not occur, or rarely occur, in democracies where public opinion matters to governments. Kofi Annan has said that human rights and development are intimately linked. Where do political rights and social rights begin and end, or intersect? The Human Rights Council is the place for that debate.

A productive global discussion is also long overdue on the rights of women, an issue that bridges the political-social divide and has been given priority by the new human rights commissioner, Navanethem Pillay. As the United Nations moves toward the 2015 finish line of its ambitious Millennium Development Goals, it becomes clearer each year that without women's participation in decision-making, economic activity and political influence, most of the goals will not be achieved. Yet in many nations women suffer low social status and enjoy scant protection, even when appropriate laws are in place. Making decisions about matters as basic as family size are often denied them, which contributes to severe poverty from the home to the national level.

Violators Must Be Isolated

The greatest achievement of an effective Human Rights Council would be the education and isolation of violators, including those with tarnished reputations who shamelessly seek council seats. Much hope is riding on a new system called universal periodic review, which will be used to examine the records of all 192 U.N. member countries in rotation, at the rate of 16 a year, whether or not they aspire to council membership. (The United States is not due for review until 2010.) Judge Arbour said the system should put all nations on an equal footing, if international panels of reviewers can be impartial. Naming and shaming does not always result in better behavior by governments. But it may be the only weapon the council will have at its disposal, and it must be used credibly.

The world mirrored in the Human Rights Council is a 21st-century reality that is not going to change. The developing nations have an unbeatable majority globally as well as in the United Nations, and richer industrial countries will have to work harder at engaging the "global South" in every international forum. Nothing good can come from confrontation, least of all in the Human Rights Council.

| "Rather than advancing the cause of human liberty, the Council is providing cover for the oppressors and persecutors."

The UN Human Rights Council Is Hypocritical

Doug Bandow

The United Nations Human Rights Council is hypocritical because many of the nations that belong to the council regularly violate the rights of their citizens, Doug Bandow opines in the following viewpoint. According to Bandow, the consistent violations of nations such as Cuba are ignored by council members from China, Egypt, and other repressive regimes. He concludes that the United States and other nations that are serious about human rights should leave the council because it is unlikely that the body will ever advance the cause. Bandow is a senior fellow at the Cato Institute, a libertarian think tank.

As you read, consider the following questions:

1. According to Bandow, how much time does the council spend debating the human rights record of every nation?

2. According to a report quoted by Bandow, what two religious groups are particularly oppressed in Cuba?

3. According to the author, what does the United Nations blame for Cuba's development problems?

The United Nations and human rights do not belong in the same sentence. Last Wednesday [June 10, 2009,] the UN Human Rights Council praised Cuba's human rights achievements. The Council was far more concerned about the U.S. embargo against Cuba than the Cuban government's brutality towards its own people.

The UN long has claimed to represent the greatest aspirations of humanity, running back to the Universal Declaration of Human Rights, which was approved more than six decades ago. But the UN's Commission on Human Rights routinely embarrassed the "international community." Often dominated by human rights abusers, the body routinely whitewashed oppressive governments and spent much of its time attacking Israel. It was one of Turtle Bay's [the Manhattan neighborhood where the UN is located] finest comedy clubs—only the performances were underwritten by U.S. taxpayers.

[In 2006] the Commission was replaced by the Human Rights Council in a vain attempt to improve operations. The [George W.] Bush administration refused to dignify the body with America's presence, but in March [2009] the Barack Obama administration announced its decision to return. Doing so obviously was a mistake.

The membership list reads like a Who's Who of repressive regimes: Angola, Egypt, Gabon, China, Jordan, Saudi Arabia, Azerbaijan, Russia, and Cuba. Many of the other members have lesser human rights problems. Authoritarian states have an obvious incentive to go easy on their fellow autocracies. Even worse, these member governments view violating human rights as *a positive good* and one of the chief responsibilities of government (in their hands, at least).

As part of its commitment to human rights, the Council conducts an annual review—which culminates in *a three hour debate* on the nation's human rights record. Strangely, these reviews seem a bit, shall we say, superficial?

Cuba's Abysmal Record

Cuba's record isn't hard to assess. The State Department helpfully summarizes the Cuban record in its annual human rights report:

> The government continued to deny its citizens their basic human rights and committed numerous, serious abuses. The government denied citizens the right to change their government. At year's end there were at least 205 political prisoners and detainees. As many as 5,000 citizens served sentences for "dangerousness," without being charged with any specific crime. The following human rights problems were reported: beatings and abuse of detainees and prisoners, including human rights activists, carried out with impunity; harsh and life-threatening prison conditions, including denial of medical care; harassment, beatings, and threats against political opponents by government-recruited mobs, police, and State Security officials; arbitrary arrest and detention of human rights advocates and members of independent professional organizations; denial of fair trial; and interference with privacy, including pervasive monitoring of private communications.

The group Freedom House ranks Cuba at the bottom in both political rights and civil liberties. "Although the degree of repression has ebbed and flowed over the past decade, the neutralization of organized political dissent remains a regime priority," explains Freedom House.

Freedom House compiles a special report on freedom of the press and, not surprisingly, ranks Cuba as "not free" in this category as well. There was some relaxation of repression [in 2008], but "Cuba continued to have the most restrictive laws on free speech and press freedom in the hemisphere." Moreover, "state security agents continued to threaten, arrest, detain, imprison, and restrict the right of movement of local and foreign journalists throughout the year."

Cuba also is one of the worst violators of religious liberty. [In 2008], explained the State Department in its annual International Religious Freedom Report: "The government continued to exert control over all aspects of social life, including religious expression. Certain groups, particularly Seventh-day Adventists and Jehovah's Witnesses, faced significant harassment and maltreatment." Although repression had eased of late, "The Ministry of the Interior continued to engage in efforts to control and monitor religious activities and to use surveillance, infiltration, and harassment against religious groups, religious professionals, and laypersons." [In May 2009] the United States Commission on International Religious Freedom placed Cuba on its Watch List since "Within this reporting period, the government expanded its efforts to silence critics of its religious freedom policies and crack down on religious leaders whose churches operate outside of the government-recognized umbrella organizations for Protestant denominations."

An Absurd Debate

There are worse offenders, of course. Compare any country against Burma or North Korea and even the worse human rights offender looks pretty good. But Cuba's record could not survive the most cursory review by a serious body. Unfortunately, the Human Rights Council is not a serious body.

The UN issued an official press release summarizing the debate, if it can be called that, on Cuba and two other states (Saudi Arabia and Cameroon):

> In the discussion on Cuba, speakers said Cuba had withstood many tests, and continued to uphold the principles of objectivity, impartiality and independence in pursuance of

Muslim Nation Views on the UN and Human Rights

Do you agree with giving the UN the authority to go into countries in order to investigate violations of human rights?

	Favor	Oppose	Not sure/Decline
Azerbaijan	77	11	12
Egypt	51	49	0
Indonesia	71	14	15
Iran	54	22	25
Nigerian Muslims	79	18	3
Turkey	47	25	28
Average	63	23	14

TAKEN FROM: "Views of the UN in Majority-Muslim Nations," WorldPublicOpinion.org, December 3, 2008.

the realization of human rights. Cuba was and remained a good example of the respect for human rights, including economic, social and cultural rights. The Universal Periodic Review of Cuba clearly reflected the progress made by Cuba and the Cuban people in the protection and promotion of human rights, and showed the constructive and responsive answer of Cuba to the situation of human rights. Cuba was the victim of an unjust embargo, but despite this obstacle, it was very active in the field of human rights. The trade, financial and economic blockade by the United States should be brought to an end, as it was the primary obstacle to the full development of Cuba.

In short, the problem is not the brutality of the Castros' regime. It is the American trade embargo—counterproductive in my view, but ignored by everyone else and actually used by the Cuban government to enhance its control. As my Cato Institute colleague Juan Carlos Hidalgo put it, "This is not from [satirical newspaper] *The Onion*, but the UN."

However, the Council summary does not do the debate justice. Pakistan wished Cuba well in realizing "all human rights for all citizens." Venezuela (you don't have to be a member to comment) lauded "the iron will" of Cuba's government. Russia said, "Cuba had taken a serious and responsible approach." Uzbekistan "stressed Cuba's work in the promotion of human rights." China declared that "Cuba had made important contributions to the international human rights cause." Egypt opined that "Cuba's efforts were commendable." And so it went.

Again, this is not from the pages of *The Onion*. It is from a debate before the Human Rights Council.

Needless to say, the Cuban government was pleased. The Cuban Interests Section (which acts as Havana's de facto embassy) put out a press release headlined: "Cuba recognized in the Human Rights Council." Havana grandly announced that it was accepting most of the Council's recommendations, and "reaffirmed its commitment to the strengthening of international cooperation on human rights issues and to the UN Human Rights Council, which must be based on the principles of universality, objectivity, impartiality and non-selectiveness."

The Council Supports Oppression

Is there some way, in theory, in which the Human Rights Council might help advance the cause of human rights? Perhaps, but it certainly is not apparent how that might be. The official "Report of the Working Group on the Universal Periodic Review" of Cuba was as stomach-churning as the ensuing debate. Rather than advancing the cause of human liberty, the Council is providing cover for the oppressors and persecutors. . . .

After receiving its UN whitewash, the Cuban government exclaimed: "The exemplary achievements of the Cuban Revolution in relation to human rights have been acknowledged once again by the international community. It has not been possible to silence the truth."

Rather than going back into the Council, the U.S. and other serious states should make a quick exit. The problem is not Cuba. It is the UN. Saudi Arabia, too, received gentle treatment. Up the next day were Azerbaijan and China—the latter of which praised the records of Cuba, Saudi Arabia, and Cameroon. This incestuous process will continue, day after day, at the expense of the rest of us.

Human rights. United Nations. Never shall the twain meet, except in a tiresome comedy routine in an expensive club operating out of a famed high-rise in New York's Turtle Bay.

| "UN forces have . . . been deployed along troubled borders . . . where their presence has helped dampen violence."

The United Nations Has Had Success in Peacekeeping

Joshua Muravchik

In the following viewpoint, Joshua Muravchik asserts that United Nations peacekeeping forces have had numerous successes in nations such as El Salvador, Mozambique, and Cambodia; however, he also acknowledges that in some situations the UN has wrongly received credit for achievements that belong to the United States. Muravchik concludes that while UN peacekeeping is not always completely successful, it has helped dampen violence and could do more if it had additional troops. Muravchik is a scholar at the School of Advanced International Studies at Johns Hopkins University and the author of several books, including The Imperative of American Leadership.

As you read, consider the following questions:

1. What group tried to disrupt peaceful elections in Cambodia, according to Muravchik?

2. As explained by the author, why does a RAND study consider Afghanistan and Iraq to be U.S. failures?

3. According to Muravchik, how many UN peacekeeping missions were carried out between 1989 and 2004?

While the UN's failures are more numerous and easier to enumerate, the organization has some successes to its credit. As against the body's failures in various conflict situations, its peacekeeping efforts in Namibia, Cambodia, El Salvador, Mozambique, Eastern Slavonia, and East Timor are generally regarded as having achieved their missions. These were cases of agreed transfers of authority, or where previously warring parties had reached a settlement but still felt distrust of one another. UN peacekeepers were not there to enforce agreements but to provide good offices trusted by all sides, verifying to each that the other was keeping its side of the bargain, or to maintain order and safety during a transition. In addition, the UN generally played a short-term administrative role that included, as a RAND [a global policy think tank] study summarized it, "disarmament, demobilization, and reintegration; encouraging political reconciliation; holding democratic elections; and overseeing the inauguration of a new national government."

An important exception to the generalization that these peacekeeping operations proceeded in environments that were already peaceful was Cambodia, where the peacekeepers found they had a tougher assignment [in 1991–1993]. Although the four main parties to the conflict reached agreement to hold elections, the most murderous, the Khmer Rouge, soon reversed itself. It announced its refusal to participate and attempted to disrupt the voting through violence and threats. Thus, the peacekeepers had to guard the balloting by force as best they could, and on the whole they succeeded admirably, aided by the surprising determination of the Cambodian populace not to be intimidated from voting. Another exception was East Timor [in 1999], where UN forces came ashore in the wake of serious mayhem that had claimed a thousand lives. But the murderous militias and Indonesian military forces responsible for the killing apparently received orders to back down in the face of the formidable Australian-led international force, and it was able to occupy the territory without taking any casualties.

A Better Success Rate than the United States?

In assessing these missions, the RAND study argues that the UN has a "better . . . success rate" at "nation-building" than the United States, a conclusion that is sure to be widely repeated. But the cases compared are dissimilar, and many are ongoing. For instance, RAND counts Afghanistan and Iraq as U.S. failures because they have not yet reached their goals.

It is also hard to understand how RAND categorizes cases, since the United States and the UN both were present in many of these situations. In one case, RAND places El Salvador in the UN column and rates it a success. But the UN was active in El Salvador only during the relatively easy endgame, after the guerrillas had agreed to lay down arms, whereas the United States spent years nurturing a "third force" in that country between the military and the guerrillas, which was the key to the success of nation-building.

On the other hand, RAND counts Somalia as a nation-building failure, as it surely was, and places it in the U.S. column. It is true that the military operation that ended in debacle for U.S. forces in Mogadishu was planned and commanded by Americans. But the idea of going beyond famine relief to nation-building in Somalia belonged to the UN, not the United States, although the United States went along. Thus, the strained comparison that RAND goes out of its way to make seems intended for polemical purposes.

Modest Successes for Peacekeepers

UN peacekeepers have also been deployed in countries in turmoil, mostly in Africa—notably Sierra Leone, Liberia, and Congo—where they have had, at best, modest accomplishments. Although the UN forces have not been strong enough to impose peace in any of these places, their presence in at least some has ameliorated problems. (In Sierra Leone, the UN intervention was initially a fruitless humiliation in which, as in Bosnia, the peacekeepers themselves were taken hostage; but a more robust British-led force operating at first outside of UN command had a better result.)

Unarmed or lightly armed UN forces have also been deployed along troubled borders, such as between Ethiopia and Eritrea, Israel and Lebanon, Israel and Syria, and Greek and Turkish Cyprus, where their presence has helped dampen violence.

A Useful Framework

The deficiencies of UN peacekeeping efforts must be judged in light of the rapid proliferation of such missions with the end of the Cold War. In the era from 1948 to 1988, there was a total of fifteen UN peacekeeping missions. In the next fifteen years there were another forty-four. Without superpower rivalry, it became much more feasible politically to introduce UN forces. This rapid upsurge in demand, however, outstripped the institution's capacities and the numbers of properly prepared troops. Hence, UN missions were typically undermanned and underequipped due to the reluctance of the advanced countries to supply soldiers for such operations. According to the UN Department of Peacekeeping Operations, the total number of Americans serving UN peacekeeping missions on May 31, 2005 was ten (as well as 19 military observers and upwards of 300 civilian police). All too often, the countries that do contribute troops bring to the table much less in the way of military capability. This is the key factor that has prevented an effective response to, for example, the humanitarian catastrophe in Darfur [Sudan] in recent times.

Notwithstanding the severe limitations, the UN does provide a useful framework for legitimizing peacekeeping missions, usually in situations in which no major power has a vested interest, and the stakes in human life are large.

"United Nations peacekeeping operations, like all mechanisms of foreign
and security policy, are imperfect."

The United Nations'
Peacekeeping Efforts
Need Improvement

Richard Williamson

*In the following viewpoint, Richard Williamson argues that
while the United Nations has operated several successful peacekeeping missions, reforms are necessary if the United States is to
continue to rely on the UN's assistance. According to Williamson, the United States must understand and acknowledge the
limits of the UN. Furthermore, he contends, peacekeeping missions should meet certain criteria, such as flexibility, better training of peacekeepers, and time limits on missions. In Williamson's
view, these and other reforms will help make the UN a greater
aid to the United States. Williamson, now a professor at North-
western University, has served as an ambassador to the UN
Commission on Human Rights, an assistant secretary of state,
and a special envoy to Sudan.*

Richard Williamson, "Testimony Before the House Foreign Affairs Committee," Congressional Hearing Transcript Database, July 30, 2009. Copyright © 2009 Federal News Service. Reproduced by permission.

As you read, consider the following questions:

1. What is the first reform suggested by Williamson?

2. As stated by the author, how big is the UN peacekeeping budget?

3. What does Williamson believe to be the most important determinant of a successful peacekeeping operation?

The U.N. is useful—it deserves engagement and support— but there is plenty of room for reform. Similarly, U.N. peacekeeping operations are helpful for burden sharing. They have an acceptance and legitimacy and capacity that has served us well in many instances.

Some have been very successful, such as Sierra Leone, Timor-Leste, Liberia and others, and some have a decidedly mixed result, including in Sudan with both UNMIS [United Nations Missions in Sudan], which failed to act appropriately to stop the destruction of Abiye in May 2008, and UNAMID [African Union/United Nations Hybrid operation in Darfur], which still faces many difficulties.

Leadership is very important. And let me note that Under-secretary Generals Alain LeRoy and Susana Malcorra, the undersecretaries for Peacekeeping and Field Support, have both brought a bigger enthusiasm and creativity to their new positions.

And let me note that there needs to be a recognition that some risk-taking is desirable, especially in field support. Failure to take some risk to make sure the equipment and other support is provided results in greater risk to the peacekeepers in the political process.

UN Peacekeeping Is Imperfect

United Nations peacekeeping operations, like all mechanisms of foreign and security policy, are imperfect. There are times peacekeeping is very useful. There are times they deserve the support. And there are times they need reform. And let me just quickly go though a list of reforms I would urge the committee to consider as it deals with ongoing peacekeeping operations.

One, the United States must be realistic about what a peacekeeping mission can do, the limits of its capacity. There are limits of available peacekeepers from contributing countries. There are limits to available equipment such as helicopters with night vision.

There are limits to political leverage and influence of the United Nations, especially when dealing with deeply entrenched sovereign governments. These limits and others must be understood, acknowledged, and be part of the analysis of whether or not to support authorization of any new peacekeeping mission.

Two, the United States must be steely-eyed and crystal clear in assessing the real support within the Security Council for any new mission. Both political will and material support is required not only at the launch of a peacekeeping operation, but it must be sustained throughout, especially if one or more of the Security Council permanent members have direct interest in the conflict or with one party of a conflict.

The effectiveness of the peacekeeping operation can be compromised on various fronts. In such situations, the likelihood of success is substantially limited.

Three, the United States should not be so anxious to launch a peacekeeping mission that it accepts inadequate mandates for too small a force size to get the job done.

Four, peacekeeping ought not to be immortal. Some peacekeeping interpositional forces, such as in Cyprus and Western Sahara, were deployed in acute situations that over time have calmed down. The dispute is resolvable but the pain on either side is not acute enough to compel compromise.

Allegations Against Peacekeepers

In recent years, there have been several harrowing reports of crimes committed by U.N. personnel, from rape to the forced prostitution of women and young girls, the most notorious of which involved the U.N. Mission in the Democratic Republic of Congo. Indeed, allegations and confirmed incidents of sexual exploitation and abuse by U.N. personnel have become depressingly routine with allegations being reported in Bosnia, Burundi, Cambodia, Congo, Guinea, Haiti, Kosovo, Liberia, Sierra Leone, and Sudan. The alleged perpetrators of these abuses include U.N. military and civilian personnel from a number of U.N. member states involved in peace operations and from U.N. funds and programs. The victims are refugees—many of them children—who have been terrorized by years of war and look to the U.N. for safety and protection.

Brett Schaefer, The Heritage Foundation, February 13, 2007.

Flexibility and Conformity

The status quo may not be preferable, but it is acceptable. The peacekeepers allow comfort to set in and unresolved issues remain unresolved, due in part to the peacekeepers themselves. [If that happens,] we should move forward and look at which peacekeeping missions should be withdrawn to force the parties to resolve it.

Five, peacekeeping must be more flexible.

Six, there has to be a recognition that in difficult environments, a lead country can be very useful, such as the United Kingdom, with the peacekeepers in Sierra Leone, and France in Cote D'Ivoire.

Seven, there needs to be reform of the work program of the U.N. Fifth Committee. That body spends an entire year on the U.N. regular budget of approximately $3 billion. However, it devotes only one month, the month of May, to the U.N. peacekeeping budget of almost $8 billion.

Eight, U.N. peacekeeping operations, like other U.N. bodies and mechanisms, should conform to the highest standards of procurement and management. Unfortunately, since such standards are not always met, to ensure appropriate oversight and accountability, the U.N. Office of Internal Oversight Services should be supported politically and financially.

Nine, progress must be made to standardize peacekeeping equipment, especially common communication systems, throughout the system.

Selection and Training Reforms

Ten, often the most important determinant of a successful peacekeeping operation is the special representative of the secretary general [SRSG] and the deputy SRSG. The personality, energy, drive, political skill, commitment, innovation and overall talent of the SRSG and deputy SRSG can be critical. There should be a more rigorous selection process imposed on both the secretary general and the Security Council.

Eleven, similarly, peacekeeping force commanders often are picked because of nationality and politics, not competence. This must end.

Twelve, there should be common training for peacekeepers, whatever their country of origin, a common procedure manual and practice.

Thirteen, progress has been made but more is required for peacekeeping activities to be integrated with the World Food Programme and other important U.N. humanitarian agencies.

And, fourteen, there needs to be better training and monitoring of peacekeepers on human rights, especially exploitation of women and children and HIV/AIDS.

Periodical Bibliography

The following articles have been selected to supplement the diverse views presented in this chapter.

Morton Abramowitz and Thomas Pickering — "Making Intervention Work," *Foreign Affairs*, September-October 2008.

Anne Bayefsky — "You Can't Say That," *Weekly Standard*, October 4, 2009.

Economist — "A Caterpillar in Lipstick? The UN's Human Rights Council," March 4, 2006.

Blaise Godet — "Reforming Human Rights: Challenges Facing New Human Rights Council," *Harvard International Review*, January 2008.

Vaclav Havel — "A Table for Tyrants," *New York Times*, May 10, 2009.

Bruce Jones — "The Limits of Peacekeeping," *Los Angeles Times*, March 2, 2006.

Paul Kennedy — "U.N.: The World's Scapegoat," *Los Angeles Times*, August 21, 2006.

Neil MacFarquhar — "In Peacekeeping, a Muddling of the Mission," *New York Times*, February 11, 2009.

New Internationalist — "A Brief History of the UN," January-February 2005.

Edmund Sanders — "An Uphill Struggle for Peace in Darfur," *Los Angeles Times*, April 27, 2008.

Lauren Vriens — "Wrongs Council," *Newsweek*, September 22, 2009.

Weekly Standard — "Law of the Jungle: The Unpunished Abuses of UN Peacekeepers," April 29, 2008.

Women in Action — "UN Human Rights Council: A Step Forward or a Step Back?" August 2007.

OPPOSING
VIEWPOINTS®
SERIES

CHAPTER 2

Is the United Nations Impartial Toward the Middle East?

Chapter Preface

On December 27, 2008, following the end of a Hamas ceasefire, Israel Defense Forces (IDF) kicked off Operation Cast Lead. Consisting first of airstrikes against Hamas terrorist cells in the Gaza Strip and then ground incursions, the operation resulted in the deaths of hundreds of Gazans (the exact number being under dispute). After Operation Cast Lead concluded, the UN Human Rights Council criticized Israel's actions and established a commission to determine whether human rights had been violated. The commission's findings were published in the so-called Goldstone Report, named for commission head Richard Goldstone, and accused both Israel and Hamas of war crimes and Israel with the further charge of "possible crimes against humanity." Not surprisingly, those on both sides of the Israeli-Palestinian conflict disagree on the fairness of the report.

Critics of the report allege that it ignored the ongoing attacks on Israel by Hamas and the IDF's concerted efforts to warn Palestinian civilians of airstrikes so that they would have time to find shelter. In particular, they charge that the UN's bias against Israel, especially in the Human Rights Council, meant that it was virtually impossible for Israel to receive a fair hearing. In remarks made following the release of the report in November 2009, Israeli ambassador to the UN Gabriela Shalev opined: "The report . . . makes explosive charges against Israel, yet the evidence provided to support such accusations is at best uncorroborated, and at worst false."

Meanwhile, supporters of the report argue that it offered a fair assessment of Israel's actions during Operation Cast Lead. In their view, Israel did wrongfully and disproportionately target civilians in its efforts to wipe out Hamas terrorists. They believe that the UN and its Human Rights Council were right to apportion Israel the greater share of the blame. As Nathan

Guttman writes in *Washington Report on Middle East Affairs*: "The U.N. committee stressed that Israel's fault was in not distinguishing between civilians and military targets as part of 'a deliberately disproportionate attack designed to punish, humiliate and terrorize a civilian population.'"

The Middle East has long been a hotbed of controversy, and the United Nations is not immune to this acrimony. In the following chapter, the authors debate whether the UN is impartial when it tackles the issues facing this incendiary region.

❚ *"UN bias against Israel is overt."*

The United Nations Is Biased Against Israel

UN Watch

The anti-Israel and anti-Semitic attitude of the United Nations is a serious problem UN Watch asserts in the following viewpoint. According to UN Watch, the United Nations has become "Ground Zero" for modern anti-Semitism, with the Human Rights Council particularly guilty of bias against Israel. In addition, UN Watch argues, the UN constantly passes anti-Israel resolutions while the actions of repressive regimes are completely ignored. UN Watch is a nongovernmental organization that monitors the performance of the United Nations, particularly regarding whether it treats its member nations—especially Israel— equally.

As you read, consider the following questions:

1. What event in 1973 strengthened the anti-Israel campaign, according to UN Watch?

2. Why does the author believe that the UN's constant censuring of Israel affects all citizens?

3. In the 2006 to 2007 session, how many resolutions did the UN General Assembly pass regarding the genocide in Darfur, as stated by UN Watch?

An alien observing the United Nations' debates, reading its resolutions, and walking its halls could well conclude that a principal purpose of the world body is to censure a tiny country called Israel.

Four Decades of Demonization

Beginning in the late 1960s, the full weight of the UN was gradually but deliberately turned against the country it had conceived by General Assembly resolution a mere two decades earlier. The campaign to demonize and delegitimize Israel in every UN and international forum was initiated by the Arab states together with the Soviet Union, and supported by what has become known as an "automatic majority" of Third World member states.

The campaign reached new strength in the wake of the Arab oil embargo of 1973, when many African states were pressured into severing relations with Israel. In 1975, following a steady drumbeat of anti-Israel declarations pushed through the International Women's Year Conference in Mexico and then the Organization of African Unity, the majority of the General Assembly adopted the "Zionism is Racism" resolution. At the same time, it instituted a series of related measures that together installed an infrastructure of anti-Israel propaganda throughout the UN. Years later, after strenuous efforts by democratic forces, the infamous resolution was repealed.

However, the legacy of 1975 remains fully intact: UN committees, annual UN resolutions, an entire UN bureaucratic division, permanent UN exhibits in New York and Geneva headquarters—all dedicated to a relentless and virulent propaganda war against the Jewish state. Together, they have made the UN into Ground Zero for today's new anti-Semitism, which is the irrational scapegoating of Israel with the true intended target being Jews. Not only do these anti-Israel measures incite hatred against Israelis and Jews everywhere, but they have done not a thing to help the Palestinian situation. On the contrary: they give strength and succor to extremists.

Paradoxically, one of the greatest violators of the UN Charter's equality guarantee has been the UN body charged with establishing and enforcing international human rights, the Human Rights Council.

Unfair and Obsessive Criticisms

The UN's discrimination against Israel is not a minor infraction, nor a parochial nuisance of interest solely to those concerned with equal rights of the Jewish people and the Jewish state. Instead, the world body's obsession with censuring Israel at every turn directly affects all citizens of the world, for it constitutes (a) a severe violation of the equality principles guaranteed by the UN Charter and underlying the Universal Declaration of Human Rights, and (b) a significant obstacle to the UN's ability to carry out its proper mandate.

None of this means Israel should be above the law. Every country, including every democracy, commits human rights violations, and states should be held to account accordingly, both domestically and internationally. Yet Israel does have the right to be treated equally under the law. The UN Charter and the rules of natural justice demand no less. It is legitimate for UN bodies to criticize Israel, but not when they do so unfairly, selectively, massively, sometimes exclusively, and always obsessively.

Likewise, it is perfectly legitimate to call attention to the rights of the Palestinian people and their often difficult conditions. But it is something else entirely to abuse their cause for the sole objective of scapegoating Israel and the Jewish people.

Signe Wilkinson Editorial Cartoon used with the permission of Signe Wilkinson and the Washington Post Writers Group in conjunction with the Cartoonist Group.

The UN Ignores Atrocities

The countless anti-Israel resolutions and related debates consume an astonishing proportion of the UN community's precious resources. This year, during the 61st Session of the General Assembly (2006–2007), the time spent by ambassadors on enacting the 22nd anti-Israel resolution of the year was time not spent on passing a single resolution on Sudan's genocide in Darfur. Diplomats at foreign ministries or UN missions have a limited amount of time to devote to any particular UN session. Because every proposed UN resolution is subjected to intensive review by various levels and branches of government, a direct result of the anti-Israel texts is a crippling of the UN's ability to tackle the world's ills.

UN bias against Israel is overt in bodies such as the General Assembly, which each year passes some nineteen resolutions against Israel and none against most other member states, including the world's most repressive regimes. The World Health Organization, meeting at its annual assembly in Geneva [Switzerland] in 2005, passed but one resolution against a specific country: Israel was charged with violating

Palestinian rights to health. Similarly, the International Labour Organization, at its annual 2005 conference in Geneva, carried only one major country-specific report on its annual agenda—a lengthy document charging Israel with violating the rights of Palestinian workers.

In the summer of 2004, the UN's International Court of Justice at The Hague issued an advisory opinion that followed the script of a political campaign orchestrated by the PLO [Palestine Liberation Organization] representative at the UN, Nasser al-Kidwa. The busiest corridor of the *Palais des Nations*, the European headquarters of the UN in Geneva, displays no less than ten larger-than-life panels devoted to the Palestinian cause.

The clear message, that the Palestinians are the world's greatest human rights victim; the clear implication, that Israel is the world's greatest human rights abuser.

There are three special UN entities dedicated to the Palestinian cause. The oldest is the Special Committee to Investigate Israeli Practices Affecting the Human Rights of the Palestinian People and Other Arabs of the Occupied Territories, created in 1968. In 1975, the General Assembly added the Committee on the Exercise of the Inalienable Rights of the Palestinian People. Supporting its work is the Division for Palestinian Rights. Lodged within the UN Secretariat, the Division boasts a sixteen-member staff and a budget of millions, which it devotes to the constant promotion of anti-Israel propaganda throughout the world.

Although Secretary-General Kofi Annan has made important pronouncements against anti-Semitism, and even—before a Jerusalem audience—against some aspects of the UN's anti-Israel bias, his regular statements on the Arab-Israeli conflict are disproportionately critical of Israel. Senior aide Lakhdar Brahimi publicly described Israel as a country whose policy constitutes "the great poison in the region."

UN Credibility Undermined

The anti-Israel apparatus within the UN, therefore, is of considerable magnitude, and cripples the functioning of the organization. The overt bias practiced against one state undermines the UN's credibility and integrity. Anyone who truly cares about the UN must take action to end this gross injustice and criminal distraction from world pandemics such as disease and poverty. Given the current period of UN reform, now is the time. Many more UN officials, member states, NGOs [nongovernmental organizations], and others need to speak out and actively oppose this longstanding inequality.

"At the United Nations, the United States has supported resolutions condemning anti-Semitism both at the General Assembly and at the UN Commission on Human Rights."

The United Nations Is Not Anti-Israel

U.S. Department of State

In the following viewpoint, the U.S. Department of State contends that there is a growing amount of anti-Semitism in the contemporary world. The report details many organizations that have been working to fight the current anti-Semitic sentiment— among them, the United Nations. The viewpoint claims that the United Nations has taken many measures to combat anti-Semitism and the United States has supported resolutions within the U.N. to condemn anti-Semitism as well. The U.S. Department of State is an executive department responsible for international relations.

U.S. Department of State, "Report on Global Anti-Semitism," January 5, 2005. Reproduced by permission.

As you read, consider the following questions:

1. According to the article, what is the most effective vehicle for a multinational approach to the anti-Semitism problem?

2. What is one of the two measures mentioned in this viewpoint that the United Nations took to fight against anti-Semitism?

3. What branches of government along with nongovernmental organizations "constitute an important partnership in continuing the vital effort to . . . stop anti-Semitism"?

Anti-Semitism is a global problem that requires a coordinated multinational approach. Thus far, the most effective vehicle for international cooperation has been the OSCE [Organization for Security and Cooperation in Europe], comprised of 55 participating states from Europe, Eurasia and North America plus Mediterranean and Asian partners for cooperation. The OSCE organized two groundbreaking conferences on anti-Semitism—in June 2003, in Vienna and in April 2004, in Berlin. These were the first international conferences to focus high-level political attention solely on the problem of anti-Semitism. The Vienna Conference identified anti-Semitism as a human rights issue.

OSCE Foreign Ministers gave further high-level political acknowledgment to the seriousness of anti-Semitism at their December 2003 meeting in Maastricht. There they took the formal decision to spotlight the need to combat anti-Semitism by deciding to task the OSCE's Office of Democratic Institutions and Human Rights (ODIHR) to serve as a collection point for hate crimes information. ODIHR is now working with OSCE member states to collect information on hate crimes legislation and to promote "best practices" in the areas of law enforcement, combating hate crimes, and education.

ODIHR established a Program on Tolerance and Non-Discrimination and now has an advisor to deal exclusively with the issue.

At their December 2004 meeting in Sofia, OSCE Foreign Ministers welcomed the Chair-in-Office's decision to appoint three special representatives for tolerance issues, including a special representative for anti-Semitism, to work with member states on implementing specific commitments to fight anti-Semitism. In addition, the Foreign Ministers accepted the Spanish Government's offer to host a third anti-Semitism conference in June 2005 in Cordoba.

The United Nations Fights Anti-Semitism

The United Nations also took important measures in the fight against anti-Semitism. One was a June 2004 seminar on anti-Semitism hosted by Secretary-General Kofi Annan. Another measure was a resolution of the United Nations Third Committee in November 2004, which called for the elimination of all forms of religious intolerance, explicitly including anti-Semitism.

Education remains a potentially potent antidote for anti-Semitism and other forms of intolerance. Following the first Stockholm Conference in 1998, convoked out of concern for the decreasing level of knowledge of the Holocaust particularly among the younger generation, Sweden, the United Kingdom and the United States decided to address the issue collaboratively. The Task Force for International Cooperation on Holocaust Education, Remembrance, and Research (ITF) emerged from this initial effort.

Today the ITF, an informal international organization operating on the basis of consensus, and without a bureaucracy, consists of 20 countries. ITF member states agree to commit themselves to the Declaration of the Stockholm International Forum on the Holocaust and to its implementation. Current members of the ITF include Argentina, Austria, Czech Republic, Denmark, France, Germany, Hungary, Israel, Italy, Latvia, Lithuania, Luxembourg, the Netherlands, Norway, Poland, Romania, Sweden, Switzerland, United Kingdom, and the United States. In addition, four other countries (Croatia, Estonia, Greece, Slovakia) maintain a liaison relationship with the ITF.

U.S. Government Actions to Monitor and Combat Anti-Semitism

The U.S. government is committed to monitoring and combating anti-Semitism throughout the world as an important human rights and religious freedom issue. As President [George W.] Bush said when he signed the Global Anti-Semitism Review Act on October 16, 2004, "Defending freedom also means disrupting the evil of anti-Semitism."

Annually, the U.S. Department of State publishes the International Religious Freedom Report and the Country Reports on Human Rights Practices. Both detail incidents and trends of anti-Semitism worldwide. The State Department's instructions to U.S. Embassies for the 2004 Country Reports on Human Rights Practices explicitly required them to describe acts of violence against Jews and Jewish properties, as well as actions governments are taking to prevent this form of bigotry and prejudice.

In multilateral fora, the Department of State called for recognition of the rise of anti-Semitism and the development of specific measures to address it. The Department played a leading role in reaching agreement in the OSCE to hold . . . two conferences on combating anti-Semitism. . . . Former New York City Mayors Rudolph Giuliani and Edward Koch led the United States delegations to the conferences in Vienna and Berlin, respectively. Each brought a wealth of knowledge and experience in fostering respect for minorities in multicultural communities. Key NGOs [nongovernmental organizations] worked productively with the Department to prepare for these conferences. In his address to the Berlin Conference, Secretary [of State Colin] Powell said: "We must not permit anti-Semitic crimes to be shrugged off as inevitable side effects of inter-ethnic conflicts. Political disagreements do not justify physical assaults against Jews in our streets, the destruction of Jewish schools, or the desecration of synagogues and cemeteries. There is no justification for anti-Semitism." At the United Nations, the United States has supported resolutions condemning anti-Semitism both at the General Assembly and at the UN Commission on Human Rights.

An important lesson of the Holocaust is that bigotry and intolerance can lead to future atrocities and genocides if not addressed forcefully by governments and other sectors of society. The United States is committed to working bilaterally to promote efforts with other governments to arrest and roll back the increase in anti-Semitism. President Bush affirmed that commitment during his visit to Auschwitz-Birkenau in 2003, stating: "This site is a sobering reminder that when we find anti-Semitism, whether it be in Europe, in America or anywhere else, mankind must come together to fight such dark impulses."

The United States Fights Anti-Semitism

U.S. Embassies implement this commitment by speaking out against anti-Semitic acts and hate crimes. Ambassadors and other embassy officers work with local Jewish communities to encourage prompt law enforcement action against hate crimes. In Turkey, the U.S. Embassy worked closely with the Jewish community following the November 2003 bombing of the Neve Shalom Synagogue. In the Middle East, our embassies have protested to host governments against practices that have allowed their institutions to promote anti-Semitism, such as the heavily watched television series "Rider Without a Horse" and "Diaspora" that respectively promoted the canard [false and derogatory story] of the blood libel [the false accusation that religious minorities murder children in religious rituals],

Progress at the UN

Israeli diplomats have been appointed to various positions at the U.N.:

- In June 2007, for the first time in the organization's history, an Israeli official was selected to head one of its committees. Rony Adam, head of the Israeli Foreign Ministry's U.N. department, was chosen to head the U.N. Committee for Program and Coordination. Adam was unanimously elected to the post after serving as the committee deputy director. The committee is comprised of 33 countries, some of which have no diplomatic relations with Israel, such as Iran, Cuba and Indonesia.

- In July 2005, Israel was elected to the deputy chairmanship of the United Nations Disarmament Commission, a subsidiary body of the GA [General Assembly].

- In June 2005, Dan Gillerman, Israel's Ambassador and Permanent Representative to the U.N., was appointed to be one of the 21 vice presidents of the GA, marking the first time an Israeli had been chosen for this position since Abba Eban in 1953. Israel's candidacy as vice president of the GA was put forth by the Western European and Others Group (WEOG), the regional group to which it belongs.

Anti-Defamation League, "Israel at the UN:
Progress Amid a History of Bias,"
September 2008. www.adl.org.

and "The Protocols of Elders of Zion [a 1903 anti-semitic publication]." U.S. bilateral demarches were effective in specific instances, but more remains to be done to encourage national leaders to speak out forcefully against anti-Semitism and in support of respectful, tolerant societies.

Building on the success achieved to date, the Department of State is accelerating its efforts with its partners globally to improve both monitoring and combating anti-Semitism in three specific areas: education, legislation, and law enforcement. The Department will continue to promote the development of Holocaust education curricula and teacher training programs. A successful program in this area has been summer teacher training partially funded through U.S. Embassies in cooperation with the Association of American Holocaust Organizations (AHO) and the United States Holocaust Memorial Museum (USHMM). At the October 2004 OSCE Human Dimension Meeting, the United States and France hosted a seminar on methodologies for teaching the Holocaust in multicultural societies. The United States also supports the work of NGOs in promoting educational programs abroad, in part based on successful seminars in the United States that teach respect for individuals and minority groups. Additionally, the U.S. State Department has supported efforts to promote tolerance in the Saudi educational system including by sponsoring the travel of religious educators to the United States to examine interreligious education.

The roots of anti-Semitism run deep and the United States does not underestimate the difficulty of reversing the recent resurgence of this ancient scourge. The legislative and executive branches, together with NGOs, constitute an important partnership in continuing the vital effort to find creative ways to monitor, contain, and finally stop anti-Semitism.

| "The inequality and injustice of the treatment of Israel becomes most obvious in comparison with the U.N.'s treatment of human-rights violations elsewhere in the world." |

The United Nations Must Fight Anti-Semitism

Anne Bayefsky

In the following viewpoint, Anne Bayefsky asserts that the United Nations has too often allowed attacks on Israel and Jews. She contends that it is ignorant not to make the connection between the discrimination of individual Jews and discrimination against the Jewish state. Anne Bayefsky is a visiting professor at Touro and Metropolitan Colleges in New York and a senior fellow at the Hudson Institute.

As you read, consider the following questions:

1. What does Bayefsky claim the United Nations is a "willing vehicle" for, as stated in the article?

2. According to the author, the U.N. General Assembly held an emergency session to condemn Israel for what?

Anne Bayefsky, "Fatal Failure: The U.N. Won't Recognize the Connection Between Anti-Zionism and Anti-Semitism," *National Review Online*, November 30, 2004. Reproduced by permission.

3. According to Bayefsky, are double standards applied only to Israel?

Last June [2004], the United Nations held its first-ever conference on anti-Semitism. Though the organization's very raison d'etre rises from the ruins of Auschwitz and Belsen, it has never produced a single resolution dedicated to combating anti-Semitism or a report devoted to this devastating global phenomenon. For those who saw light at the end of the tunnel, this week the prospect of enlightenment at the General Assembly came to an inglorious conclusion. One mention of "anti-Semitism" made it into one paragraph of a general resolution on religious intolerance. Fifty-four U.N. states—of the 153 members that cast votes—refused to support even that.

What's going on? Let's connect the dots. Immediately before voting against concern for anti-Semitism, the same countries refused to support a call for governments "to ensure effective protection of the right to life . . . and to investigate . . . all killings committed for any discriminatory reason, including sexual orientation." Anti-Semitism and killing people because of their sexual orientation are acceptable to almost every one of the 56 members of the Organization of the Islamic Conference (OIC).

The resolution involving killing homosexuals is only one of many U.N. human-rights resolutions in which the OIC stands with the violator, not the victim. The real question is: How do they get away with it, let alone pass themselves off as seriously interested in human rights, including those of Palestinians?

Arab and Muslim states unabashedly take the offensive, hijacking the medium of human rights to serve a political agenda aimed at denying Jewish self-determination and destroying the Jewish state—the ultimate form of anti-Semitism. The willing vehicle for such a heist is the United Nations. The U.N.'s June [2004] anti-Semitism conference served to invigorate their well-versed two-track approach: Put the Jews on one side, Israel on the other, and divide and conquer.

Uh, Germany. . .

Track One works this way. Over the last three months the possibility of a U.N. resolution dedicated to anti-Semitism has been under discussion. A full-fledged resolution offers the potential of serious examination of the phenomenon, including new forms of anti-Semitism with the Jewish state as its victim. The battle associated with presenting a new and substantive stand-alone anti-Semitism resolution, however, scared off every democratic U.N. member state. The next idea was to have the European Union (EU) sponsor a resolution on anti-Semitism modeled on the Berlin Declaration, which was adopted in April by the Organization for Security and Co-operation in Europe (OSCE). The OSCE had eked out: ". . . international developments or political issues, including those in Israel or elsewhere in the Middle East, never justify anti-Semitism." Europeans could not quite bring themselves to say that terrorism aimed at ethnically cleansing Israel of Jews was also a form of anti-Semitism. But the Berlin Declaration's mention of the word "Israel" in the context of "anti-Semitism" put Arab and Islamic states at the U.N. on the warpath (yet another one).

Some hoped the Germans would take a leadership role in campaigning for a specific anti-Semitism resolution at the General Assembly. In true gangland style, Germany was soon given to understand that such a role would jeopardize its hoped-for permanent seat on the Security Council, and any sense of historical responsibility vanished. Nor was any other EU member prepared to confront Arab and Muslim opposition. More sympathetic EU-wannabe states were afraid to annoy the EU gatekeepers. The U.S. State Department was content to leave the matter to European initiative (or lack thereof).

And given that an Israeli-sponsored resolution has virtually no chance of being passed at the General Assembly, Israel chose not to go it alone.

Climbing way down the ladder, efforts turned to a general resolution on religious intolerance. One proposal would have included in the preamble the words "welcoming the Berlin Declaration" of the OSCE. But Berlin contained the dreaded reference to "Israel." Hence, despite the declaration's European parentage, the proposal was rejected by the European Union on the grounds that Arab and Islamic states said no. Then began EU-OIC negotiations, which weaken and debilitate so many U.N. outcomes. References to Islamophobia and Christianophobia and language accommodating all other religions were added. Islamophobia was taken out of alphabetical order and put first before anti-Semitism. And there the EU finally made its stand. The OIC still balked, but their efforts to defeat the reference failed. They had, however, successfully managed to reduce it to a single mention, and to exclude the Berlin reference and any other detail that might have connected anti-Semitism with Israel.

In the meantime, the U.N. Commission on Human Rights will soon receive another annual report on Islamophobia and the "situation of Muslim and Arab peoples in various parts of the world." It continues to adopt annual resolutions expressing "deep concern at . . . intolerance and discrimination in matters of religion or belief" that mention only Islam.

The Demonization of Israel

Now for Track Two and the demonization of Israel. In the intervening five months since the one-day U.N. conference on anti-Semitism ended, the U.N. anti-Israel campaign was ramped up. The U.N.'s judicial organ, the International Court of Justice, decided in July that Israel's security fence violated its version of international law. The contortions necessary to arrive at this conclusion resulted in a decision that there is no right of self-defense under the U.N. Charter when terrorists are not state actors. But just in case anyone missed the point, Judge Tanaka spoke of "the *so-called* terrorist attacks by Palestinian suicide bombers against the Israeli civilian population" (emphasis added) and Judge Elaraby (Egyptian ambassador to the U.N. until 1999) affirmed a "right of resistance" on the grounds, judicially speaking of course, that "violence breeds violence."

The U.N. General Assembly held another emergency session in July to condemn Israel for building a wall to prevent terrorism, but not to name and condemn Palestinian terrorists, their Palestinian Authority patrons, or their state sponsors. This fall [2004], another 20 anti-Israel resolutions are in the process of adoption at the regular session of the General Assembly. Another of the annual U.N.-sponsored NGO [nongovernmental organization] conferences "in support of the Palestinian people" was held at U.N. Headquarters in September. Participants studied "such sterile paradigms as 'Israel's self-defence,'" how to "promote a sporting, cultural and economic boycott" of Israel, and "to challenge Christian Zionism in moderate Christian communities." A damage register was created for alleged victims of Israel's security fence, but nothing for victims of Palestinian terrorism. The chief of UNWRA (the United Nations Relief and Works Agency), Peter Hansen, gave a spirited defense of employing Hamas members.

Three more reports of U.N. "experts" were produced for the General Assembly taking direct aim at Israel. One expert has a mandate only to address human-rights violations by Israel in the territories and not Palestinian human-rights violations in Israel. He started this year's report by analogizing Israel to apartheid South Africa, despite the fact that Arab states have virtually purged themselves of Jews, while in Israel the 20 percent Arab population enjoys more democratic rights than anywhere in the Arab world. The U.N. expert on the right to food focused on a concocted Israeli-driven humanitarian food crisis in the territories, but refused to say a single word about the millions going hungry in Zimbabwe because of discrimination and manipulation of the country's food shortages to punish political opponents. And then there was the expert report on racism and xenophobia that blamed Israel for the rise of anti-Semitism, but that was still studying whether "alleged" ethnic motivations had anything to do with the genocide and displacement of more than a million people in the Darfur region of Sudan.

Israel Blamed for Human-Rights Abuses

The inequality and injustice of the treatment of Israel becomes most obvious in comparison with the U.N.'s treatment of human-rights violations elsewhere in the world. A U.N. General Assembly resolution on Iran could only be adopted last week [November 2004] after any notion of creating a single investigator into human-rights abuse in that country was eliminated. No resolution was even attempted on countries like China, where 1.3 billion people are without basic civil and political rights, or Saudi Arabia, where gross discrimination against women is endemic and more than a million female migrant workers are essentially slaves. Resolutions put forward on Sudan and Zimbabwe were prevented this week from even coming to a vote. The grand total of the GA's 2004 country-specific criticism of human-rights violations around the globe in the 190 U.N. members, excluding Israel: One resolution for each of the Democratic Republic of the Congo, Iran, Myanmar, and Turkmenistan. It was on November 24 [2004] that the U.N. General Assembly defeated action on Sudan and Zimbabwe. Simultaneously, U.N. delegates in the adjoining room adopted nine resolutions condemning Israel.

The record is incontrovertible: double-standards applied only to Israel; the lack of interest in states with much worse human-rights records; and the resulting demonization of Israel through overt manipulation of human-rights rhetoric and mechanisms. Even the underlying anti-Semitism becomes plain with the overt attempt to eliminate concern with anti-Semitism.

And still the self-appointed human-rights professionals claim they don't get it. In the latest effort to rend Jews from the state of Israel a new formula has emerged. Taking objection to anti-Semitism in the form of egregious discrimination against the Jewish state is said to be motivated by a desire to eliminate any criticism of Israel. As Ken Roth, executive director of Human Rights Watch, told the *Jerusalem Post* on November 4, "There is a cottage industry of people out there who try to accuse of bias those who criticize Israel's human-rights record not because the criticisms are unwarranted but as a way of simply defending Israel from any criticism." Reading from the same script, Mary Robinson, the former U.N. high commissioner for human rights, in a lecture at Brown University on November 7, worried about "blur[ing] the line between anti-Semitism and legitimate criticism of Israel. . . . [S]ome . . . regard any criticism of Israel as anti-Semitic." But "Israel's supporters" should not, said Robinson, "use the charge of anti-Semitism to stifle legitimate discussion." Similarly, Esther Benbassa, an invitee to a November 11–13 U.N. meeting in Barcelona that was convened to advise the U.N.'s expert on racism and xenophobia, has complained of "the dangerous phase of intimidation" that "eagerly sees behind each word, each gesture, and each criticism of Israeli policy, an anti-Semite."

Failure to Acknowledge the Connection

What an incredible outrage. A cursory glance at the newspapers in the democratic state of Israel, or the decisions of its vibrant judiciary, or the myriad discussions, conferences, and writings of Jews across the globe reveal a cacophony of public and self-driven criticism. The failure to acknowledge the deep connection between discrimination and demonization of individual Jews and discrimination and demonization of the Jewish state is not just ignorant—it is lethal. This failure also answers the original question of how Arab and Muslim states, and all those who have jumped on the Arafat bandwagon, pass themselves off as interested in human rights rather than the defeat of Jewish self-determination.

In a 1968 appearance at Harvard, Martin Luther King said, "When people criticize Zionists, they mean Jews. You are talking anti-Semitism." But Martin Luther King would not find a home at the United Nations or its allied nongovernmental human-rights organizations.

> *"Long ago UNRWA schools became hot-beds of anti-Western, anti-American, and anti-Semitic indoctrination, and recruiting offices for terrorist groups."*

The UN Relief and Works Agency Promotes Terrorism

Asaf Romirowsky

In the following viewpoint Asaf Romirowsky argues that the United Nations Relief and Works Agency (UNRWA) operates Palestinian refugee camps and schools that are hotbeds of terrorist activity. He contends that UNRWA-run schools indoctrinate students with anti-American and anti-Semitic teachings and that the agency holds back Palestinians from improving and rebuilding their lives. According to Romirowsky, this makes the UNRWA refugee camps very different from the camps operated by the United Nations High Commission on Refugees. Romirowsky is the international relations liaison officer to Jordan of the Israel Defense Force and an adjunct scholar at the Middle East Forum in Philadelphia.

As you read, consider the following questions:

1. What changes does Romirowsky say James Lindsay levels against UNRWA?

2. According to the author, who dominates local UNRWA offices?

3. How should U.S. tax dollars be spent, in Romirowsky's view?

Debates just aren't what they used to be. A case in point, on April 24 [2009] the Woodrow Wilson International Center for Scholars in Washington, D.C. presented a panel discussion entitled "UNRWA at 60: The United Nations and the Palestinian Refugees." The event was co-sponsored with the United Nations Relief and Works Agency (UNRWA) and Friends of UNRWA.

The notice posted on the Wilson Center's website promised those attending the talk would be presented with a "panel [that] will offer participants the opportunity to debate one of the most interesting foreign policy subjects. The 60th anniversary of UNRWA is an occasion to reflect upon the contribution that the Agency has made to the prosperity and stability of the Middle East. UNRWA has served four generations of Palestinian refugees."

A One-Sided Debate

The panelists were Karen Koning AbuZayd, Commissioner-General, UNRWA; Ali Abunimah, Palestinian-American journalist; and Philip C. Wilcox, Jr., President, Foundation for Middle East Peace. The moderator was former U.S. diplomat Aaron David Miller, now a Public Policy Scholar at the Woodrow Wilson Center and is considered by most accounts to be a far leftist Jewish scholar sympathetic towards the Palestinian cause.

Alas, this was a one-sided discussion on a highly politicized topic by distinguished advocates for maintaining the status of Palestinians as everlasting refugees maintained by UNRWA.

It is obviously a concern that the Wilson Center, a reputable academic institution that prides itself on being nonpartisan, would host such a one-sided debate.

Enter James Lindsay, who served as a legal advisor for UNRWA from 2000 to 2007 and as the general counsel from 2002. In his role, he oversaw all UNRWA legal activities, from aid contracts to relations with Israel, Jordan, Syria, Lebanon, and the Palestinian Authority.

Until recently, Lindsay was the Aufzien fellow at the Washington Institute for Near East Policy and under their auspices he published a report entitled *Fixing UNRWA: Repairing the UN's Troubled System of Aid to Palestinian Refugees*. This is the first time an UNRWA insider has broken the code of silence and exposed the problems of the organization from within. Lindsay's report warns that UNRWA has deteriorated dramatically since its establishment. Among other charges Lindsay states that UNRWA offers services to those who [are] not actually in need of them; "No justification exists for millions of dollars in humanitarian aid going to those who can afford to pay for UNRWA services."

Had the Wilson Center sought out Lindsay then we would have been presented with a more evenhanded presentation, possibly even an actual debate. After some back and forth with the organizers, it was not to be.

UNRWA Enables Political Radicalism

Anyone who knows something about UNRWA and the call for a Palestinian right of return knows that this discussion within the academic hallways is based on a highly specific reading of history, one that assumes an Israeli responsibility for creating

A Palestinian-Run Organization

At UNRWA, more than 99% of the staff are local Palestinians. They sit at the many local levers of the UNRWA distribution machinery, which under UNRWA policy takes on the coloration of and yields to the policies of host governments—as UNRWA officials explained to U.S. lawmakers who some years ago challenged the use of anti-Israeli textbooks in UNRWA schools.

In today's terrorist-run Gaza, such an approach carries exactly the kind of deadly implications now playing out.

Claudia Rosett, Forbes.com, January 8, 2009.

the refugee problem via "ethnic cleansing." Restitution from the allegedly guilty party involves the return of the refugees and their descendants.

To an outsider, UNRWA seems a humanitarian group helping Palestinian refugees. In reality, it helps destroy the chances of Arab-Israeli peace, promotes terrorism, and holds Palestinians back from rebuilding their lives.

Long ago UNRWA schools became hotbeds of anti-Western, anti-American, and anti-Semitic indoctrination, and recruiting offices for terrorist groups. The vast majority of UNRWA's employees are Palestinian, and local offices are dominated by radicals who staff and subsidize radical groups while potentially intimidating anyone from voicing a different line. UNRWA facilities are used to store and transport weapons, and have actually served as military bases.

In this process, UNRWA has broken all the rules that are presumed to govern humanitarian enterprises, encouraging their resettlement, avoiding political stances, and putting refugees in danger. But by design, UNRWA is the exact opposite of other refugee relief operations, such as those orchestrated by the United Nations High Commissioner on Refugees [UNHCR]. UNHCR seeks to resettle refugees; UNRWA is dedicated to blocking resettlement in favor of the "right of return."

UNHCR helps refugees to restore normal lives elsewhere so that they can move on with their existence; UNRWA's role is to ensure Palestinian lives remain abnormal, inevitably filled with anger and a thirst for revenge that inspires violence and which can only be quenched by a victorious return. UNHCR tries to create stable conditions for refugees; UNRWA's de facto mission is to enable radical political activity and indoctrination by armed groups which ensures a continual state of near chaos.

UNRWA Is a Liability

Furthermore, if we are truly concerned about the well-being of Palestinian society there are a few things we should strive for. Now that more and more policy-makers and individuals are aware of UNRWA's problems, how do we significantly decrease the hold UNRWA has on Palestinian society? If we are to work towards improving the environment in which Palestinians reside and work towards the creation of institutions that will foster civil society and promote some element of democratization, all the services UNRWA currently provides to the Palestinians should be handed over to parallel agencies within the UN, who already provide duplicate services for other UN beneficiaries. Gradually weaning Palestinians off UNRWA and moving the inter-dependency from UNRWA to the Palestinian Authority must be the ultimate goal.

UNRWA in its current configuration is a liability for many reasons. For one, by granting its employees U.N. diplomatic status, it undercuts the organization's accountability. Too many UNRWA workers have abused their diplomatic privilege to engage in or encourage terrorism. Television crews have filmed

UNRWA employees escorting armed Palestinian fighters in U.N. vehicles. Agency-operated—and, by extension America-funded—schools decorate their classrooms with flags and banners celebrating terrorist groups. All this must stop if we ever want to see any kind of change in addition to calling for accountability as well as checks and balances from those agencies we finance.

A principal policy issue for the United States will be how to aid in mobilizing donors, both public and private, for a financial infusion of aid resources to finance refugee compensation (and resettlement, immigration, and rehabilitation) as well as the permanent status agreement in general. All of this must be done outside the UNRWA framework.

All and all, our tax dollars would be better spent promoting independent Palestinian organizations and private-sector growth. UNRWA does not work towards a resolution. In fact, the opposite is true. UNRWA perpetuates the problem.

I "*UNRWA is not in the business of hiring terrorists.*"

The UN Relief and Works Agency Does Not Support Terrorism

Maya Rosenfeld

The United Nations Relief and Works Agency (UNRWA) does not encourage terrorist activity, Maya Rosenfeld argues in the following viewpoint. According to Rosenfeld, a variety of false claims have been made about the UNRWA, including that it hires terrorists and oversees schools that teach hatred of Israel. Instead, Rosenfeld contends, Israel has been a consistent supporter of UNRWA, and the agency has helped Palestinian refugees become more self-sufficient. Rosenfeld is a research fellow at the Truman Institute, an organization dedicated to fostering peace and cooperation in the Middle East.

As you read, consider the following questions:

1. According to the author, when was the only time that UNRWA installations were misused?

Maya Rosenfeld, "UNRWA: Setting the Record Straight," un.org/unrwa, January, 2009. Copyright © 2009 United Nations. Reprinted with the permission of the United Nations.

2. What did a commission that studies Palestinian Authority textbooks find, as stated by Rosenfeld?

3. In the author's view, why is it not feasible to replace the
UNRWA with the UN High Commission for Refugees?

In January 2009 James Lindsay produced a report entitled
*Fixing UNRWA: Repairing the UN's Troubled System of Aid
to Palestinian Refugees* for The Washington Institute for Near
East Policy. The report contained a number of misleading al-
legations against UNRWA [United Nations Relief and Works
Agency]. . . .

*"UNRWA is complicit in terrorism because it turns a blind
eye to militant activity in 'its' camps".*

UNRWA does not run refugee camps. It is a UN agency
with a clearly defined mandate, in accordance with which, it
provides health, education and other humanitarian services to
refugees, only one third of whom live in refugee camps. The
Agency has never been given any mandate to administer, su-
pervise or police the refugee camps or to have any jurisdiction
or legislative power over the refugees or the areas where they
lived. The Agency has no police force, no intelligence service
and no mandate to report on political and military activities.
This responsibility has always remained with the host countries and Israel, who maintained law and order, including
within refugee camps.

Between 1967 and 1994, the Israeli authorities were in
charge of security and law and order in the West Bank and
Gaza Strip, including the 19 refugee camps in the West Bank
and the eight in Gaza Strip. Subsequently, and based on Israel's
bilateral agreements with the Palestinian Authority and the
terms of the Oslo Accords, responsibility for security and law
and order in area "A" (including all eight camps in Gaza and
12 of those in the West Bank) was passed to the Palestinian
Authority. Under the same accords, the remaining seven camps

in the West Bank in areas "B" and "C", and in the Israel-defined Greater Jerusalem, remain to this day under Israel's security control.

"Many of UNRWA's installations have been turned into bomb making factories".

The Agency is scrupulous about protecting its installations against misuse by any person or group and conducts constant inspections to ensure that its rules are complied with. Only once in 52 years has there been credible evidence that UNRWA installations have been put to misuse and that was in 1982 in Lebanon in the midst of the civil war. The Agency immediately launched an internal inquiry and discovered that the training centre in Siblin had indeed been misused for a brief period prior to June 1982 during a time when governmental authority was absent in south Lebanon. The investigation was handled in an open and transparent fashion and prompt action was taken to remedy the situation. Both Israelis and Palestinians accepted the objectivity of the inquiry and the efficacy of the Agency's subsequent action.

From 1967 to-date, UNRWA has not received from the Government of Israel any complaint related to the misuse of any of its installations in the West Bank and Gaza Strip.

UNRWA Does Not Hire Terrorists

"UNRWA employs Hamas members on its payroll" and therefore "supports terror".

UNRWA is not in the business of hiring terrorists. It has in place very strict standards of conduct and it expects all of its area and international staff members to adhere to them. These are contained in the Agency's extensive "Staff Rules and Regulations". UNRWA enforces a zero-tolerance policy towards inappropriate activities of its staff members, which is applied irrespective of where or when those activities take place.

UNRWA applicants are vetted during the recruitment process by personnel departments. Moreover, the Agency adheres to strict standards of conduct concerning the impartiality of staff members in the discharge of their professional duties, which are well documented. Swift disciplinary action is taken whenever there is evidence of involvement of staff members in inappropriate political activities or in military activities. Such actions are well-known, predictable and consistent, and therefore deter others.

The Staff Rules and Regulations quoted above are consistent with the relevant norms for all international civil servants.

In short UNRWA cannot police the beliefs of its staff, but its does strictly police their behaviour.

"Hamas is in control" of UNRWA's Area Staff Union.

UNRWA's Area Staff do have a union, but it is not staffed by representatives of any militant or political group or party, nor are elections to the union conducted on party or factional lists. Needless to say, all members of UNRWA's Area Staff Union are subject to the rules and regulations quoted above concerning impartiality in the discharge of their duties as UN staff.

UNRWA "does nothing" to ensure staff impartiality.

To ensure that Area staff are made aware of the obligations imposed upon them by the Staff Regulations, all new staff have to sign that they have "been made acquainted with and accept the conditions laid down in the staff regulations and rules". In addition, the Commissioner-General has on numerous occasions reminded UNRWA's area and international staff of their obligations of impartiality as UN employees and officials. In numerous letters to all staff he has recalled that "staff of the Agency are required to conduct themselves in accordance with established principles and practices of the United Nations and must not engage in any activity which is incompatible with their status as independent and impartial civil servants". He also stated that "whilst UNRWA staff members, like other United Nations officials, are entitled to their political views, such views must not be allowed to come into conflict with the duty of the individual staff member to give loyal service uninfluenced by external political pressures".

In addition, since the start of the current strife the Agency has employed a group of International Staff as Operational Support Officers one of whom's main tasks is to ensure the integrity of UNRWA property and installations in the OPT [Occupied Palestinian Territories]. The Agency enforces all the rules mentioned above in a stringent manner and has initiated disciplinary measures against its staff where necessary. For example, the Agency once disciplined a staff member for attending a political rally in contravention of Staff Rules and Regulations. On another occasion, a staff member was disciplined for having circulated an email with inappropriate political connotations.

"UNRWA spends American tax dollars without any kind of oversight".

U.S. law (section 301 (c) of the Foreign Assistance Act) prohibits US contributions to UNRWA from assisting refugees who have engaged in any act of terrorism. A recent US Government Accounting Office (GAO) investigation conducted in 2003 found no instance of UNRWA failing to comply with that law.

The UNRWA and Anti-Semitism

"UNRWA schools and textbooks teach hatred of Israel".

The curriculum in the Agency's schools is determined by the education authorities in the locations where it operates. For historical reasons UNRWA schools followed the Jordanian curriculum in the West Bank and the Egyptian curriculum in the Gaza Strip and this practice continued under the Israeli control of those areas between 1967 and 1994. Since 1994 the

Focus on Human Development

Today UNRWA maintains records for 771,000 refugees registered with us in the West Bank [WB]. They make up approximately 30% of the WB population of 2.3 million.

Of these we provide services in a regular way to approximately 600,000.

Our focus and mandate is human development programming: primary health care, elementary education, and relief and social services for the most vulnerable. We also manage three vocational training centres for unemployed youth. We also operate a small hospital and a small teacher-training facility.

UNRWA, States News Service, *March 22, 2010.*

Palestinian Authority [PA] has progressively been replacing the old Jordanian and Egyptian textbooks as new PA-produced textbooks become available.

The United States Congress requested the US Department of State to commission a reputable NGO [nongovernmental organization] to conduct a review of the Palestinian curriculum. The Israel/Palestine Center for Research and Information (IPCRI) was thereby commissioned by the US Embassy in Tel Aviv and the US Consul General in Jerusalem to review the PA's textbooks. Its report was completed in March 2003 and delivered to the State Department for submission to Congress. Its Executive Summary states: "The overall orientation of the curriculum is peaceful despite the harsh and violent realities on the ground. It does not openly incite against Israel and the Jews. It does not openly incite hatred and violence. Religious and political tolerance is emphasized in a good number of textbooks and in multiple contexts."

Nathan Brown, Professor of Political Science at George Washington University, has also published studies on this subject. Regarding the Palestinian authority's new textbooks, he states:

- "The new books have removed the anti-Semitism present in the older books

- while they tell history from a Palestinian point of view, they do not seek to erase Israel, delegitimize it or replace it with the 'State of Palestine'

- each book contains a foreword describing the West Bank and Gaza as 'the two parts of the homeland'

- the maps show some awkwardness but do sometimes indicate the 1967 line and take some other measures to avoid indicating borders; in this respect they are actually more forthcoming than Israeli maps

- the books avoid treating Israel at length but do indeed mention it by name

- the new books must be seen as a tremendous improvement from a Jewish, Israeli, and humanitarian view

- they do not compare unfavorably to the material my son was given as a fourth grade student in a school in Tel Aviv".

Ruth Firer of Hebrew University reached similar conclusions in her study of the new books.

Much of the criticism of Palestinian textbooks has been based on research published by an organisation entitled the "Centre for Monitoring the Impact of Peace", CMIP. The organisation's work has been criticised as "tendentious and highly misleading" by Professor Brown.

"UNRWA does nothing to teach tolerance and understanding in its schools".

The Agency has been creating curriculum enrichment materials for teachers and extra-curricular activities for students focusing on peace education, human rights, tolerance and conflict resolution since long before the issue of its textbooks became a subject for public debate. In 1999 it stepped up this effort when it undertook a comprehensive review of all the books used in its schools that led to a donor-funded special project to promote tolerance, human rights and conflict resolution. These systematic efforts, which have included translations into Arabic of relevant textbooks, the creation of special manuals and involvement in cross-community summer camps, have reached every one of the Agency's schools in the West Bank and Gaza. The Agency's work in this area has been praised by, among others, the Israeli delegation to the United Nations.

"The Government of Israel does not support UNRWA".

Israel has consistently supported the work of UNRWA over the decades and the Agency depends on close co-operation with the Israeli authorities to carry out its operations in the territory that came under Israel's control in 1967. At that time Israel specifically requested UNRWA continue its operations in the West Bank and Gaza Strip and entered into an agreement committing it to facilitate the work of the Agency. The Government of Israel has made many statements of support for UNRWA over the years, for example, Israel's Ambassador to the UN, Yosef Lamdan's statement to the UN Fourth Committee on 4 November 1999 affirmed: "We see in UNRWA a major force for stability among a significant segment of Palestinian society." On 30 October 2000, Israel's representative to the UN, David Zohar, said: "UNRWA has continued to play an important role . . . in administering a variety of important services, especially in the fields of health care and education. At this time Israel would like to formally record its appreciation for this good work under the able leadership of Commissioner General P. Hansen."

UNRWA Must Continue Its Role

"UNRWA perpetuates rather than solves the Palestine refugee problem".

It has long been recognised that a solution to the Palestine refugee problem requires a political settlement among the parties involved. UNRWA was established to cater to the humanitarian needs of the refugees pending such a political settlement. Removing UNRWA from the scene would not cause the refugee issue to disappear, but it would lead to untold suffering and hardship. The UN resolution that established the Agency clearly recognised the need for humanitarian relief to Palestine refugees both to prevent "conditions of starvation and distress" and to "further conditions of peace and stability". Removing that humanitarian relief could only do further damage to the stability of the region.

UNRWA has always looked forward to a time when the relevant political parties would bring about a situation where there would be no more need for the Agency. Following the signing of the Oslo Accords, and the emergence of hope that a solution was in sight, the Agency began preparing itself for the eventual hand-over of its services to the Palestinian Authority and the other host governments. The Agency wanted to be ready for the possibility that there would be a just and lasting settlement of the refugee problem. Unfortunately however, the peace process has faltered and all relevant parties to the conflict have stressed the need for UNRWA to continue its services.

"UNRWA could be replaced by the United Nations High Commission for Refugees".

UNRWA and the UNHCR are both UN agencies mandated by the international community to do specific jobs for refugee populations. UNRWA deals specifically with Palestine refugees and their unique political situation. One reason for the distinction is that in the main the UNHCR is mandated to offer refugees three options, namely local integration, resettle-

ment in third countries or return to their home country—
options which must be accepted voluntarily by refugees under
UNHCR's care. These are not feasible for Palestine refugees as
the first two options are unacceptable to the refugees and
their host countries and the third is rejected by Israel. Given
this context, the international community, through the General Assembly of the United Nations, requires UNRWA to
continue to provide humanitarian assistance pending a political solution.

"UNRWA has fostered a culture of dependency among the Palestine refugees".

Normally only 5.7 per cent of the refugee population receive food or other direct assistance from UNRWA—special
hardship cases [including families] without a breadwinner, the
elderly and the disabled. Rather than foster dependency,
UNRWA's education and healthcare services have enabled the
vast majority of the refugee population to become self-
sufficient members of the local communities. Indeed UNRWA-
educated Palestinian doctors, engineers and administrators
have made a meaningful contribution to the development of
the region as a whole.

The Agency's award-winning micro-credit programme,
which provides commercial, self-sustaining loans to the refugee community, has also furthered the cause of self-reliance
among the refugees and has placed a special emphasis on assisting female entrepreneurs. Since its inception the Microfinance and Micro-enterprise Programme has awarded 49,000
loans worth a total of over $69 million.

UNRWA's gender balanced schools and its support for
women-run community organisations have encouraged the
empowerment of Palestinian women through training, legal
advice and other assistance.

> *"The [Islamic nations'] anti-defamation campaign is itself part of a larger agenda to reshape the understanding of human rights."*

Islamic Nations Threaten UN Human Rights Principles

Luiza Ch. Savage

In the following viewpoint Luiza Ch. Savage contends that efforts by Islamic nations at the United Nations to prohibit defamation of religion are harmful because they stifle free speech and violate human rights traditions. According to Savage, this campaign has already prevented discussion at the UN Human Rights Council concerning violence against women in Muslim nations. Savage concludes that these laws are too easy to abuse and that tools are already in place to guard against religious discrimination. Savage is the Washington bureau correspondent for the Canadian magazine Maclean's.

Luiza Ch. Savage, "Stifling Free Speech—Globally: A Coalition of Islamic States Is Using the United Nations to Enact International 'Anti-defamation' Rules," *Maclean's*, vol. 121, August 4, 2008, pp. 26–30. Copyright © 2008 by Maclean's Magazine. Reproduced by permission.

As you read, consider the following questions:

1. According to the author, what was the first year Pakistan brought a defamation of religions resolution to the UN Human Rights Council?

2. What is the Organization of the Islamic Conference, described by Savage?

3. What tool does the author say already exists to protect Muslims from discrimination?

Asma Fatima, a petite, bespectacled Pakistani diplomat in Washington, sat at the front of a crowded Capitol Hill hearing room on July 18, [2008,] carefully considering whether a man seated a few places to her left on the panel should be jailed. The occasion was a panel discussion convened by a group of congressmen to educate their colleagues on the issue of religious freedom, and the man was Canadian Ezra Levant, who in February 2006 republished Danish cartoons of the Prophet Muhammad in his now-defunct magazine the *Western Standard*, which resulted in, among other things, two complaints of "discrimination" before the Alberta human rights commission. One complaint was withdrawn, but the other continues. If it is upheld, Levant could face a large fine, a lifetime order not to talk about "radical Islam" disparagingly, and be forced to issue an apology. If Levant does not comply with these orders, he could be imprisoned for contempt of court.

Fatima tried to find the right words to explain the depth of the emotions at stake. "The cartoon issue really, really hurt Muslims around the world," she told an audience that included congressional staffers as well as officials from the departments of State, Justice, and the media, and various human rights advocates, including a pair of Buddhist monks in bright robes. "There are certain things that should not be said." Ultimately, though, Fatima concluded that a journalist should be, as she put it "off the hook." Her government has not been so generous.

A Successful Suppression

Pakistan and the other nations that have banded together in the Organization of the Islamic Conference have been leading a remarkably successful campaign through the United Nations to enshrine in international law prohibitions against "defamation of religions," particularly Islam. Their aim is to empower governments around the world to punish anyone who commits the "heinous act" of defaming Islam. Critics say it is an attempt to globalize laws against blasphemy that exist in some Muslim countries—and that the movement has already succeeded in suppressing open discussion in international forums of issues such as female genital mutilation, honour killings and gay rights.

The campaign gives a new global context in which to view Levant's ordeal and other recent attempts to censor or punish Canadian commentators, publishers and cartoonists. Human rights cases were brought against this magazine [*Maclean's*] for the October 2006 publication of an excerpt of a book by Mark Steyn that, the complainants alleged, "subjected Canadian Muslims to hatred and contempt." David Harris, a former chief of strategic planning for the Canadian Security Intelligence Service, was sued for remarks he made on the Ottawa radio station CFRA linking a Canadian Islamic group to a controversial American organization. And in May [2008], a Nova Scotia Islamic group filed complaints with Halifax police and the province's human rights commission against the *Halifax Chronicle-Herald* for a cartoon it considered a hate crime.

Pakistan brought the first "defamation of religions" resolution to the UN Human Rights Council in 1999—before the attacks of 9/11 and a resulting "backlash" against Muslims. That first resolution was entitled "Defamation of Islam." That title was later changed to include all religions, although the texts of all subsequent resolutions have continued to single out Islam. The resolutions have passed the UN Human Rights Council every year since the first was introduced. In 2005, the delegate from Yemen introduced a similar resolution to the UN General Assembly, and it passed, as it has every year since, with landslide votes. In March [2008], the Islamic nations were successful in introducing a change to the mandate of the UN's special rapporteur on freedom of expression—an official who travels the world investigating and reporting on censorship and violations of free speech—to now "report on instances where the abuse of the right of freedom of expression constitutes an act of racial or religious discrimination." The issue is expected to be a focal point of the UN World Conference Against Racism [in 2009] in Geneva (a gathering Canada plans to boycott after the 2001 meeting in Durban devolved into acrimonious exchanges over Israel).

A Threat to Human Rights

The trend has rights advocates worried for numerous reasons, beginning with the language used. If the notion of "defaming" a religion sounds a little unfamiliar, that's because it is a major departure from the traditional understanding of what defamation means. Defamation laws traditionally protect individual people from being materially harmed by the dissemination of falsehoods. But "defamation of religions" is not about protecting individual believers from damage to their reputations caused by false statements—but rather about protecting a religion, or some interpretation of it, or the feelings of the followers. While a traditional defence in a defamation lawsuit is that the accused was merely telling the truth, religions by definition present competing claims on the truth, and one person's religious truth is easily another's apostasy. "Truth" is no defence in such cases. The subjective perception of insult is what matters, and what puts the whole approach on a collision course with the human rights regime—especially in countries with an official state religion.

"Islamophobia is a problem. But this is not a practical solution, and it destabilizes the human rights agenda," said Angela Wu, international law director for the Becket Fund for Religious Liberty, a public-interest law firm based in Washington that is dedicated to protecting the free expression of all religious traditions. And, she further told the congressional briefing, "The defamation of religions protects ideas rather than individuals, and makes the state the arbiter of which ideas are true. It requires the state to sort good and bad ideologies." By doing so, she said, the approach "violates the very foundations of the human rights tradition by protecting ideas rather than the individuals who hold ideas."

In a written brief, Wu said that the resolutions seek to mimic the kinds of anti-blasphemy laws that exist in countries such as Pakistan. The UN resolutions "operate as international anti-blasphemy laws and provide international cover for domestic antiblasphemy laws, which in practice empower ruling majorities against weak minorities and dissenters," her brief states. Pakistan's penal code includes a section that states that defiling Islam or its prophets is deserving of the death penalty; that defiling, damaging or desecrating the Quran will be punished with life imprisonment; and insulting another's religious feelings can be punished with 10 years in prison. A 2006 report from the U.S. State Department on international religious freedom stated that such anti-blasphemy laws "are often used to intimidate reform-minded Muslims, sectarian opponents, and religious minorities, or to settle personal scores." According to Amnesty International, Younis Masih, a Christian, was sentenced to death in 2007 for allegedly making derogatory remarks about the Prophet Muhammad. In Egypt, a professor at Cairo University was declared an "apostate" in 1995 for teaching his students to read parts of the Quran metaphorically, and was ordered to divorce his Muslim wife.

The congressional briefing also heard from Ziya Meral, a Turkish researcher and journalist who recently published a report on apostasy laws in the Middle East, documenting in horrific details the tortures, killings, and persecution not only of Christians and Jews, but of Muslims in some countries who dared question the state-endorsed views of Islam. "This has tremendous implications for millions of people around the world," Meral said at the briefing. Wu noted that the majority of victims of anti-blasphemy laws are Muslims.

The campaign is beginning to raise alarm in some corners of the UN. In March [2008], the UN's special rapporteur on the right to freedom of opinion and expression, Ambeyi Ligabo—the same one whose job has just been amended to report on the defamation of religions—compared the measures to other attempts to oppress individuals who speak out against governments. "The special rapporteur is also concerned about the trend of increasing the scope of defamation laws to include the protection of subjective values, such as a sense of national identity, religions, state symbols, institutions or even representatives such as the head of state," he wrote in his last annual report to the Human Rights Council before his term ends in August [2008]. "The special rapporteur reiterates that the provisions on protection of reputation contained in international human rights law are designed to protect individuals, not abstract values or institutions."

Criticism of Islam Has Become Taboo

A broad interpretation of defamation, Ligabo further wrote, "has more often than not been used by governments as a means to restrict criticism and silent [*sic*] dissent. Furthermore, as regional human rights courts have already recognized, the right to freedom of expression is applicable not only to comfortable, inoffensive or politically correct opinions, but also to ideas that 'offend, shock and disturb.' The constant confrontation of ideas, even controversial ones, is a stepping

Dissent Equated to Blasphemy

To those who voted for the resolution on defamation of religion, I say, believing in freedom of speech means believing in freedom of speech of views you do not like. By passing anti-blasphemy resolutions, such as these, the UN seems to expect us all to accept everything we are told to believe, because if we show dissent or express our opinions against these beliefs, we will get prosecuted as blasphemers.

Marquez Comelab,
Indian Home Educators Network,
June 3, 2009. www.ihen.org.

stone to vibrant democratic societies." Ligabo added that limits on hate speech were put into international agreements in order to prevent war propaganda and incitement of national, racial or religious hatred. They were "not designed to protect belief systems from external or internal criticism."

Yet that is exactly what they are already doing. The campaign against "defamation of religions" can already claim some impact. During a discussion at the UN Human Rights Council in June, two non-governmental organizations [NGOs] were scheduled to give a joint three-minute speech describing the widespread violence against women in Muslim countries, including "honour killings" and female genital mutilation. In his planned remarks, the NGO speaker wanted to mention the failure of Islamic religious leaders to clearly condemn the practices, and linked Islamic law, called sharia, to the stoning of adulteresses and child marriages. He was repeatedly interrupted by Egypt's delegate, who, after reading a copy of the full speech, objected. The delegate said that discussion of sharia "will not happen." Islam, he said, "will not be crucified in this council." According to a detailed report by the Reuters news organization, he asked the president of the council, a Romanian delegate, to bar any debate that included sharia because it would "amount to spreading of hatred against certain members of this council." The Romanian suspended the session and told the NGOs not to mention sharia, according to Reuters. Egypt, backed by Pakistan and Iran, said that referring to sharia law in the council meant "crucifying" Islamic states.

Louise Arbour, the former Canadian Supreme Court justice who served as the UN human rights commissioner, accused the countries of imposing "taboos" over the council. "It is very concerning in a council which should be . . . the guardian of freedom of expression, to see constraints or taboos, or subjects that become taboo for discussion," she said at a news conference. She also noted that the treatment of homosexuals, who are prosecuted as criminals in a number of Islamic countries and others, is "fundamental" to the debate on sexual discrimination around the world. "It is difficult for me to accept that a council that is the guardian of legality prevents the presentation of serious analysis or discussion on questions of the evolution of the concept of non-discrimination," Arbour said. Arbour stepped down from the post in June and was not available to discuss the incident, her spokeswoman said.

Susan Bunn Livingstone, a former U.S. State Department official who specialized in human rights issues and also spoke to the July 18 congressional gathering, said the developments at the UN are worrisome. "They are trying to internationalize the concept of blasphemy," said Livingstone at the panel. She contrasted "the concept of injuring feelings versus what is actually happening on the ground—torture, imprisonment, abuse." And, she added, "They are using this discourse of 'defamation' to carve out any attention we would bring to a country. Abstractions like states and ideologies and religions are seen as more important than individuals. This is a moral failure."

A Larger Effort to Reshape Human Rights

The fact that the resolutions keep passing, and that UN officials now monitor countries' compliance, could help the concept of "defamation of religions" become an international legal norm, said Livingstone, noting that when the International Court of Justice at The Hague decides what rises to the level of an "international customary law," it looks not to unanimity among countries but to "general adherence." "That's why these UN resolutions are so troubling," she said. "They've been passed for 10 years."

The anti-defamation campaign is itself part of a larger agenda to reshape the understanding of human rights being advanced by the Organization of the Islamic Conference, a group of more than 50 states promoting Muslim solidarity and co-operation in economic, social, and political affairs. The organization was founded and is largely funded by Saudi Arabia, a monarchy ruled under strict religious laws, where women, religious minorities and gay people are subject to various forms of discrimination and human rights abuses.

In March [2008], the group held a summit in Dakar, Senegal. Their final communiqué ran 52 pages and included a comprehensive strategy on human rights that featured a plan to shield Islamic states from being pressured to change their more contentious practices through international human rights laws and organizations. The conference expressed "deep concern over attempts to exploit the issue of human rights to discredit the principles and provisions of Islamic sharia and to interfere in the affairs of Muslim states." It also called for "abstaining from using the universality of human rights as a pretext to interfere in the internal affairs of states and undermining their national sovereignty." The states also resolved to coordinate and co-operate "in the field of human rights particularly in the relevant international fora to face any attempt to use human rights as a means of political pressure on any member state."

They also called for a binding international covenant to protect religions from defamation. The organization "stressed the need to prevent the abuse of freedom of expression and the press for insulting Islam and other divine religions, calling upon member states to take all appropriate measures to consider all acts, whatever they may be, which defame Islam, as heinous acts that require punishment." The conference also expressed its strong support for an initiative spearheaded by the king of Morocco that calls for developing an international charter that defines "appropriate standards and rules" for exercising the right of freedom of expression and opinion, and "the obligation to respect religions [*sic*] symbols and sanctities as well as spiritual values and beliefs." The states are working on an entire Islamic human rights charter.

Yet if the goal is to protect Muslims from discrimination or denunciation, the legal tools already exist. The UN International Covenant on Civil and Political Rights protects against religious discrimination. It ensures the right to freedom of thought, conscience and religion. It also protects against advocacy of religious hatred that constitutes incitement to discrimination, hostility or violence.

The U.S. Congress is beginning to pay attention to the issue. In addition to the July 18 briefing organized by the congressional task force on religious freedom, several bills have been introduced to protect the traditional definition of defamation and to preserve the traditional interpretation of free speech. One of the bills would allow Americans to counter-sue in U.S. courts against foreigners who pursue them in foreign courts for charges that would not constitute defamation under American law. Another bill would forbid U.S. courts from enforcing foreign defamation judgments unless they are consistent with the robust free speech protections in the U.S. constitution. The bills have not been voted on.

Unclear and Easy to Abuse

Meanwhile, the campaign by the Muslim states presses on. The latest Human Rights Council resolution introduced by Pakistan in March [2008] notes with deep concern, among other things, "the increasing trend in recent years of statements attacking religions, Islam and Muslims in particular, in human rights forums." It calls on states to "take actions to prohibit the dissemination" of "ideas and material aimed at any religion or its followers that constitute incitement to racial and religious hatred, hostility or violence." It also states that freedom of expression is subject to limitations, including those necessary for "national security or of public order, or of public health or morals."

Fatima, the Pakistani diplomat, advised journalists to "just avoid hurting religious sentiment." But whose religious sentiment? Those who follow traditions of Islam that forbid the depiction of Muhammad, or those who don't? Should only cartoons of the prophet be the basis for legal complaints, or also, for example, the depiction of the Prophet on the frieze inside the U.S. Supreme Court, alongside other historical lawgivers? According to the Becket Fund brief to the congressional task force, "Under the standards promoted by the 'defamation of religion' resolutions, when a Muslim states his belief that Jesus was a prophet, but not God incarnate, such statements could also be considered 'defamation' against the Christian faith of many believers."

The religious defamation laws urged by the resolutions rely on subjective emotional reactions and are therefore easy to abuse. "We don't want a jurisprudence of hurt feelings," said Wu. Levant calls the anti-defamation campaign a "soft jihad" [holy war]—an attempt to advance Islamic law around the world, not through violence but through Western legal channels. "If an army came to our shores saying give up equal rights for women and your freedom of speech, we would defend ourselves," Levant told *Maclean's* after the briefing. "But when lawyers and lobbyists come, we are confused."

Periodical Bibliography

The following articles have been selected to supplement the diverse views presented in this chapter.

Douglas Davis	"Who Is Goldstone to Judge?" *Spectator*, October 24, 2009.
Economist	"Hamas Versus the United Nations: The Struggle for Gaza," May 29, 2010.
Dan Ephron	"Man in the Middle," *Newsweek*, June 7, 2010.
Sally Fitzharris	"The Last Word," *Middle East*, December 2009.
Delinda C. Hanley	"UNRWA at 60: The U.N. and Palestinian Refugees," *Washington Report on Middle East Affairs*, July 2009.
Joseph Loconte	"The UN's Platform for Racism," *Weekly Standard*, April 22, 2009.
National Post	"Help, Not Hate," January 25, 2010.
Ruth Wedgwood	"Zionism and Racism, Again: Durban II," *World Affairs*, Spring 2009.
Ian Williams	"The Flap over Durban II: Anything but the Facts, Ma'am," *Washington Report on Middle East Affairs*, May-June 2009.
Stephen Zunes	"The Gaza War, Congress and International Humanitarian Law," *Middle East Policy*, Spring 2010.

OPPOSING
VIEWPOINTS®
SERIES

CHAPTER 3

Should the United States Support the United Nations?

Chapter Preface

From the beginning, the United States and the United Nations have shared a very special relationship. Before World War II had even ended, U.S. president Franklin Delano Roosevelt had led the way in establishing an international organization that would maintain peace and security, when he and British prime minister Winston Churchill signed the Atlantic Charter on August 14, 1941. In February 1945, Roosevelt, Churchill, and Soviet leader Joseph Stalin reiterated this intent at the Yalta Conference. When the United Nations was established in October 1945, the United States was named one of the five permanent members of the UN Security Council.

But despite its long history, the relationship between the United States and the United Nations has often been rocky. For example, in 2005, during the George W. Bush administration, the Republican-controlled House of Representatives passed a measure that would withhold America's dues from the UN unless the international body underwent a number of reforms. However, the measure failed to become law. Efforts to reduce America's financial obligation to the UN have continued since then, as critics of the UN believe the United States should not support the activities of the organization. However, supporters of the UN contend that the United States should continue to pay its full share. Writing for History News Network, Gus Feissel and Chris O'Sullivan opine, "Recent public opinion polls reveal that a majority of Americans favor the US paying its U.N. dues in full, including its peacekeeping dues, which are seriously in arrears." They also point out that the amount that the United States pays in yearly dues to the UN is far less than it spends each month in Iraq.

The United Nations would not exist without the initial support of the United States. Some say it cannot exist without continuing U.S. support. However, many people wonder if the United States should continue this long-standing relationship. The contributors to this chapter debate the connection between the United States and the UN.

"America's leaders must again say the
UN matters."

U.S. Leaders Must Support the United Nations

Mark Malloch Brown

*In the following viewpoint, Mark Malloch Brown asserts that
U.S. leaders must support the United Nations because otherwise
the UN will be unable to respond to global crises. He maintains
that inconsistent support by U.S. politicians has made it difficult
for reforms to be implemented. Brown concludes that the United
States must also recognize that the problems it faces cannot be
solved internally and that it requires global assistance. Brown is
a UN deputy secretary-general.*

As you read, consider the following questions:

1. According to Brown, how much did the United States
   spend on UN peacekeeping costs in 2006?

2. What is "stealth" diplomacy, as explained by the author?

3. What are three problems besetting the United States that
   defy national solutions, as detailed by Brown?

Mark Malloch Brown, "Address: Power and Super-Power: Global Leadership in the
Twenty-First Century," Century Foundation and Center for American Progress—
Security and Peace Initiative, June 6, 2006. Reproduced by permission of the author.

I am going to give what might be regarded as a rather un-UN speech. Some of the themes—that the United Nations is misunderstood and does much more than its critics allow—are probably not surprising. But my underlying message, which is a warning about the serious consequences of a decades-long tendency by US administrations of both parties to engage only fitfully with the UN, is not one a sitting United Nations official would normally make to an audience like this [made up of U.S. policy experts].

But I feel it is a message that urgently needs to be aired. And as someone who has spent most of his adult life in this country, only a part of it at the UN, I hope you will take it in the spirit in which it is meant: as a sincere and constructive critique of US policy towards the UN by a friend and admirer. Because the fact is that the prevailing practice of seeking to use the UN almost by stealth as a diplomatic tool while failing to stand up for it against its domestic critics is simply not sustainable. You will lose the UN one way or another.

A Core of Collective Security

Multilateral compromise has always been difficult to justify in the American political debate: too many speeches, too many constraints, too few results. Yet it was not meant to be so.

The all-moral-idealism-no-power institution was the League of Nations. The UN was explicitly designed through US leadership and the ultimate coalition of the willing, its World War II allies, as a very different creature, an antidote to the League's failure. At the UN's core was to be an enforceable concept of collective security protected by the victors of that war, combined with much more practical efforts to promote global values such as human rights and democracy.

Underpinning this new approach was a judgement that no President since [Harry] Truman has felt able to repeat: that for the world's one super-Power—arguably more super in 1946 than 2006—managing global security and development issues through the network of a United Nations was worth the effort. Yes, it meant the give and take of multilateral bargaining, but any dilution of American positions was more than made up for by the added clout of action that enjoyed global support.

Today, we are coming to the end of the 10-year term of arguably the UN's best-ever Secretary-General, Kofi Annan. But some of his very successes—promoting human rights and a responsibility to protect people from abuse by their own governments; creating a new status for civil society and business at the UN—are either not recognized or have come under steady attacks from anti-UN groups.

To take just one example, 10 years ago UN peacekeeping seemed almost moribund in the aftermath of tragic mistakes in Rwanda, Somalia and Yugoslavia. Today, the UN fields 18 peacekeeping operations around the world, from the Congo to Haiti, Sudan to Sierra Leone, Southern Lebanon to Liberia, with an annual cost that is at a bargain bin price compared to other US-led operations. And the US pays roughly one quarter of those UN peacekeeping costs—just over $1 billion this year [2006].

That figure should be seen in the context of estimates by both the GAO [Government Accountability Office] and RAND [a public policy think tank] Corporation that UN peacekeeping, while lacking heavy armament enforcement capacity, helps to maintain peace—when there is a peace to keep—more effectively for a lot less than comparable US operations. Multilateral peacekeeping is effective cost-sharing on a much lower cost business model, and it works.

That is as it should be and is true for many other areas the UN system works in, too, from humanitarian relief to health to education. Yet for many policymakers and opinion leaders in Washington, let alone the general public, the roles I have described are hardly believed or, where they are, remain discreetly underplayed. To acknowledge an America reliant on international institutions is not perceived to be good politics at home.

U.S. Leadership and Cooperation

However, inevitably a moment of truth is coming. Because even as the world's challenges are growing, the UN's ability to respond is being weakened without US leadership.

Take the issue of human rights.

When Eleanor Roosevelt took the podium at the UN to argue passionately for the elaboration of a Universal Declaration of Human Rights, the world responded. Today, when the human rights machinery was renewed with the formation of a Human Rights Council to replace the discredited Commission on Human Rights, and the US chose to stay on the sidelines, the loss was everybody's.

I hope and believe the new Council will prove itself to be a stronger and more effective body than its predecessor. But there is no question that the US decision to call for a vote in order to oppose it in the General Assembly, and then to not run for a seat after it was approved by 170 votes to 4, makes the challenge more difficult.

More broadly, Americans complain about the UN's bureaucracy, weak decision-making, the lack of accountable modern management structures and the political divisions of the General Assembly here in New York. And my response is, "guilty on all counts."

But why?

In significant part because the US has not stuck with its project—its professed wish to have a strong, effective United Nations—in a systematic way. Secretary [of State Madeleine] Albright and others here today [June 2006] have played extraordinary leadership roles in US-UN relations, for which I salute them. But in the eyes of the rest of the world, US commitment tends to ebb much more than it flows. And in recent years, the enormously divisive issue of Iraq and the big stick of financial withholding have come to define an unhappy marriage.

As someone who deals with Washington almost daily, I know this is unfair to the very real effort all three Secretaries of State I have worked with—Secretary Albright, Secretary [Colin] Powell and Secretary [Condoleezza] Rice—put into UN issues. And today, on a very wide number of areas, from Lebanon and Afghanistan to Syria, Iran and the Palestinian issue, the US is constructively engaged with the UN. But that is not well known or understood, in part because much of the public discourse that reaches the US heartland has been largely abandoned to its loudest detractors such as Rush Limbaugh and Fox News. That is what I mean by "stealth" diplomacy: the UN's role is in effect a secret in Middle America even as it is highlighted in the Middle East and other parts of the world.

Exacerbating matters is the widely held perception, even among many US allies, that the US tends to hold on to maximalist positions when it could be finding middle ground.

We can see this even on apparently non-controversial issues such as renovating the dilapidated UN Headquarters in New York. While an architectural landmark, the building falls dangerously short of city codes, lacks sprinklers, is filled with asbestos and is in most respects the most hazardous workplace in town. But the only government not fully supporting the project is the US. Too much unchecked UN-bashing and stereotyping over too many years—manifest in a fear by politicians to be seen to be supporting better premises for overpaid, corrupt UN bureaucrats—makes even refurbishing a building a political hot potato.

The Pitfalls of U.S. Support

One consequence is that, like the building itself, the vital renewal of the Organization, the updating of its mission, its governance and its management tools, is addressed only inter-

Obama Reengaging with UN

We [the United States] have also re-engaged the United Nations. We have paid our bills. We have joined the Human Rights Council. We have signed the Convention of the Rights of Persons with Disabilities. We have fully embraced the Millennium Development Goals. And we address our priorities here, in this institution—for instance, through the Security Council meeting that I will chair tomorrow on nuclear non-proliferation and disarmament, and through the issues that I will discuss today.

This is what we have already done. But this is just a beginning. Some of our actions have yielded progress. Some have laid the groundwork for progress in the future. But make no mistake: This cannot solely be America's endeavor. Those who used to chastise America for acting alone in the world cannot now stand by and wait for America to solve the world's problems alone. We have sought—in word and deed—a new era of engagement with the world. And now is the time for all of us to take our share of responsibility for a global response to global challenges.

> *Barack Obama,*
> *remarks to the UN General Assembly,*
> *September 23, 2009.*

mittently. And when the US does champion the right issues like management reform, as it is currently doing, it provokes more suspicion than support.

Last December [2005], for example, largely at US insistence, instead of a normal two-year budget, Member States approved only six months' worth of expenditure. Developing and developed countries, the latter with the US at the fore, are now at loggerheads over whether sufficient reform has taken place to lift that cap, or indeed whether there should be any links between reform and the budget. Without agreement, we could face a fiscal crisis very soon.

There has been a significant amount of reform over the last 18 months, from the creation of a new Ethics Office and whistle-blower policy, to the establishment of a new Peace-building Commission and Human Rights Council. But not enough.

The unfinished management reform agenda, which the US sensibly supports, is in many ways a statement of the obvious. It argues that systems and processes designed 60 years ago for an organization largely devoted to running conferences and writing reports simply don't work for today's operational UN, which conducts multibillion-dollar peacekeeping missions, humanitarian relief operations and other complex operations all over the world. The report sets out concrete proposals for how this can be fixed while also seeking to address the broader management, oversight and accountability weaknesses highlighted by the "oil-for-food" program [which involved alleged corruption].

One day soon we must address the massive gap between the scale of world issues and the limits of the institutions we have built to address them. However, today even relatively modest proposals that in any other organization would be seen as uncontroversial, such as providing more authority and flexibility for the Secretary-General to shift posts and resources to organizational priorities without having to get direct approval from Member States, have been fiercely resisted by the G-77, the main group of developing countries, on the grounds that this weakens accountability. Hence the current deadlock.

What lies behind this?

It is not because most developing countries don't want reform. To be sure, a few spoilers do seem to be opposed to reform for its own sake, and there is no question that some countries are seeking to manipulate the process for their own ends with very damaging consequences. But in practice, the vast majority is fully supportive of the principle of a better-run, more effective UN; indeed they know they would be the primary beneficiaries, through more peace, and more development.

Many Nations Distrust America

So why has it not so far been possible to isolate the radicals and build a strong alliance of reform-minded nations to push through this agenda?

I would argue that the answer lies in questions about motives and power.

Motives, in that, very unfortunately, there is currently a perception among many otherwise quite moderate countries that anything the US supports must have a secret agenda aimed at either subordinating multilateral processes to Washington's ends or weakening the institutions, and therefore, put crudely, should be opposed without any real discussion of whether they make sense or not.

And power, that in two different ways revolves around perceptions of the role and representativeness of the Security Council.

First, in that there has been a real, understandable hostility by the wider membership to the perception that the Security Council, in particular the five permanent members, is seeking a role in areas not formally within its remit, such as management issues or human rights.

Second, an equally understandable conviction that those five, veto-wielding permanent members who happen to be the victors in a war fought 60 years ago, cannot be seen as representative of today's world—even when looking through the lens of financial contributions. Indeed, the so-called G-4 of Security Council aspirants—Japan, India, Brazil and Germany—contribute twice as much as the P-4, the four permanent members, excluding the U.S. [British] Prime Minister Tony Blair acknowledged exactly this point on his trip to Washington [in May 2006], and it is something which does need to be addressed. More broadly, the very reasonable concerns of the full UN membership that the fundamental multilateral principle that each Member State's vote counts equally in the wider work of the UN needs to be acknowledged and accommodated within a broader framework of reform. If the multilateral system is to work effectively, all States need to feel they have a real stake.

America Must Engage with the World

But a stake in what system?

The US—like every nation, strong and weak alike—is today beset by problems that defy national, inside-the-border solutions: climate change, terrorism, nuclear proliferation, migration, the management of the global economy, the internationalization of drugs and crime, the spread of diseases such as HIV and avian flu. Today's new national security challenges basically thumb their noses at old notions of national sovereignty. Security has gone global, and no country can afford to neglect the global institutions needed to manage it.

Kofi Annan has proposed a restructuring of the UN to respond to these new challenges with three legs: development, security and human rights, supported, like any good chair, by a fourth leg, reformed management. That is the UN we want to place our bet on. But for it to work, we need the US to support this agenda—and support it not just in a whisper but in a coast to coast shout that pushes back the critics domestically and wins over the sceptics internationally. America's leaders must again say the UN matters.

When you talk better national education scores, you don't start with "I support the Department of Education." Similarly for the UN it starts with politicians who will assert the US is going to engage with the world to tackle climate change, poverty, immigration and terrorism. Stand up for that agenda consistently and allow the UN to ride on its coat-tails as a vital means of getting it done. It also means a sustained inside-the-tent diplomacy at the UN. No more "take it or leave it," red-line demands thrown in without debate and engagement.

Let me close with a few words on Darfur to make my point.

A few weeks ago, my kids were on the Mall in Washington, demanding President [George W.] Bush to do more to end the genocide in Darfur, and President Bush wants to do more. I'd bet some of your kids were there as well. Perhaps you were, too. And yet what can the US do alone in the heart of Africa, in a region the size of France? A place where the Government in Khartoum [Sudan] is convinced the US wants to extend the hegemony it is thought to have asserted in Iraq and Afghanistan.

In essence, the US is stymied before it even passes "Go." It needs the UN as a multilateral means to address Sudan's concerns. It needs the UN to secure a wide multicultural array of troop and humanitarian partners. It needs the UN to provide the international legitimacy that Iraq has again proved is an indispensable component to success on the ground. Yet, the UN needs its first parent, the US, every bit as much if it is to deploy credibly in one of the world's nastiest neighbourhoods.

Back in Franklin and Eleanor Roosevelt's day, building a strong, effective UN that could play this kind of role was a bipartisan enterprise, with the likes of Arthur Vandenberg and John Foster Dulles joining Democrats to support the new body. Who are their successors in American politics? Who will campaign in 2008 for a new multilateral national security?

"Most surely expected that our nation's leaders would always use the veto to protect America's interests, an expectation that is by no means realistic today."

The United States Should Leave the United Nations

John F. McManus

In the following viewpoint, John F. McManus contends that the United States should withdraw from the United Nations. He claims that Americans should oppose reforms to the United Nations because the removal of the veto powers would create a new world order. John F. McManus is the current president of the John Birch Society, a right-wing political advocacy group which owns American Opinion Publishing—the publisher of The New American.

As you read, consider the following questions:

1. According to McManus, where is the power in the United Nations located?

2. What are the original five permanent members of the Security Council?

John F. McManus, "UN Reform Isn't the Answer," *The New American*, January 26, 2004. Reproduced by permission.

3. What does McManus believe is the "proper response" of Americans to the cries for U.N. reform?

Flag wavers for the United Nations like to point out that nations large and small have a voice in the "world forum." For instance, Julian Hunte of minuscule Saint Lucia (population: 160,000) currently finds himself as the president of the General Assembly.

But the power in the UN doesn't reside in the General Assembly; it's located in the Security Council. Originally made up of only 11 members (four more were added in 1965), only five have ever been designated "permanent" and each of these possesses a veto over Security Council decisions. (Nonpermanent members serve for only two years, and their places are then awarded to others.) The language in the UN Charter's Article 27 states that Security Council decisions must include "the concurring votes of the permanent members." The five permanent members originally named were the Republic of China (Taiwan), France, the Soviet Union, the United Kingdom, and the United States. Two of these memberships were later transferred to the People's Republic of China and Russia.

Possession of veto power supposedly assures Americans that no Security Council resolution would ever unfavorably impact the United States. The veto power's very existence persuaded some of the senators in 1945 that there was nothing to fear by approving UN membership. Most surely expected that our nation's leaders would always use the veto to protect America's interests, an expectation that is by no means realistic today.

The Abolition of Veto Power

Still, because possession of the veto power leaves the door open for any of the five permanent members—specially the United States—to thwart UN designs, a rising number of UN partisans have suggested that it be abolished. In December

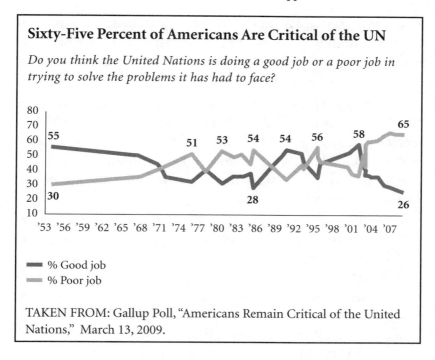

Sixty-Five Percent of Americans Are Critical of the UN

Do you think the United Nations is doing a good job or a poor job in trying to solve the problems it has had to face?

- ▬ % Good job
- ▬ % Poor job

TAKEN FROM: Gallup Poll, "Americans Remain Critical of the United Nations," March 13, 2009.

1985, for instance, World Federalist Association Vice President John Logue testified before a subcommittee of the House Foreign Affairs Committee. He stridently called for action to "reform, restructure and strengthen the United Nations." To "be able to make and enforce law on the individual," he pointedly declared, "the Security Council veto must go."

Though Logue may have been ahead of the pack, the number of those wanting to reform the UN as he suggested has grown. During a convocation at Notre Dame University in April 1991, retired President Father Theodore Hesburgh called for restructuring the UN in part by "eliminating the veto possessed by the five permanent Security Council members." An unabashed partisan of the "new world order," Hesburgh has spent much of his adult life joining and playing an important role in various globalist organizations.

In April 1996, former Soviet dictator Mikhail Gorbachev convened a gathering in Bhurban, Pakistan. Delegates to the affair produced a 12-plank "Bhurban Statement" urging that the UN "should become the principal custodian of global human security." To accomplish this goal, stated the document: "There should be no veto power."

Canadian oil billionaire and New Age heavyweight Maurice Strong has served the UN in a variety of ways, including secretary-general of the UN's 1992 "Earth Summit" and senior adviser to UN Secretary-General Kofi Annan. He has frequently called for revising the UN's structure, including the removal of the Security Council veto.

In 2000, the little-known United Nations University (UNU) produced a study offering the following conclusion: "To respect sovereignty is to be complicit in human rights violations." Formed in 1973 to assist the UN in resolving "global problems," the UNU produces recommendations such as urging the world body to "remove the Great Power veto" to facilitate its ability to sanction "humanitarian war."

In 2003, David Davenport of the supposedly conservative Hoover Institution suggested that the UN could become a "more effective decision-making body" by limiting the veto power to a requirement that "at least two nations . . . exercise it to be effective." *The Weekly Standard*, also a supposedly conservative voice, has called for eliminating the veto power.

Brookings Institution senior research analyst Parag Khanna authored an op-ed piece for the December 6, 2003 *New York Times* proposing ways to make the world body function more efficiently. Khanna wants the UN to add Japan and India to the roster of Security Council permanent members, collapse the French and British places into a single seat for the European Union, and further beef up the permanent membership by awarding slots to the Organization of American States, the League of Arab States and the African Union. "But most importantly," he wrote, "if the United States sincerely wants a more effective Security Council, it will have to relinquish its veto power in favor of majority voting."

Proper American Response

The Brookings Institution is currently led by former *Time* magazine columnist and former Deputy Secretary of State Strobe Talbott. Perhaps his most revealing utterance is that in the next hundred years "nationhood as we know it will be obsolete."

For an American, the proper response to cries for UN reform and restructuring is to demand that our nation leave the world body altogether. Even with veto power, a succession of U.S. administrations has shown little interest in using it to protect our nation's independence.

> "The United States must champion re-
> form so the United Nations can help us
> meet the challenges of the 21st century."

The United States Must Push for Reform of the United Nations

Brett Schaefer and Steven Groves

In the following viewpoint, structured as an open letter to then-president-elect Barack Obama, Brett Schaefer and Steven Groves maintain that the United Nations is too unreliable, ineffective, and susceptible to corruption to be effective. They contend that the United States must lead the way in reforming the UN. According to the authors, this reform movement should focus on the United States' financial leverage and address the UN's waste and mismanagement of resources. Schaefer and Groves conclude that a reformed UN will better serve U.S. interests. Schaefer and Groves work at the Kathryn and Shelby Cullom Davis Institute for International Studies at the Heritage Foundation, a conservative public policy research organization.

As you read, consider the following questions:

1. In the opinion of the authors, how should the United States use its financial leverage?

2. What is the "unfortunate reality" of the United Nations, according to Schaefer and Groves?

3. Which country is the largest contributor to the UN regular budget, according to the authors?

President-elect [Barack] Obama, while we may disagree with your view that the United Nations is "indispensable," we do agree that it is imperfect and in need of substantial reform. We also believe that, as President, you should never give the U.N. a veto over American action to protect American national interests.

The U.N. suffers from confused purposes, competing interests, and lopsided burden-sharing. It has shown itself to be unreliable in addressing threats to international peace and security, such as Iran and North Korea's nuclear weapons programs, and in helping to establish vibrant democracies in Iraq and Afghanistan. It has displayed an unhealthy interest in intervening in member states' domestic policies in such areas as economic regulation and legal rulings. It has been uneven and unfair as an arbiter of human rights. And it has proven to be susceptible to corruption, mismanagement, and abuse with distressing frequency.

It is time to rethink and reshape our engagement with the United Nations so that it better serves both U.S. interests and the organization's own stated purposes. Your statements indicate that you understand this.

The U.N. Must Be Reformed

We especially agree that the U.N. needs to be reformed. Noble intentions do not excuse its many failings. It has proven ineffective in bringing lasting peace and security in many places

Congress's Influence on UN Reform

Congress's influence over U.S. funding of the United Nations is a powerful tool for furthering U.S. reform policy at the United Nations. However, there may be other strategies for Congress to consider when advocating its reform agenda. These strategies . . . include, but are not limited to:

- Resolutions—Members of Congress may propose and/or enact simple or concurrent resolutions expressing an opinion, fact, or principle in one or both chambers of Congress. . . .

- Working with the U.N. Secretary-General—Some previous and current Members of Congress and Administrations have worked to earn the support of U.N. secretaries-general to help advocate their positions. Developing a relationship with the chief administrative officer of the United Nations can be valuable during some negotiations, where the Secretary-General can act as a bridge among member states. . . .

- Collaborating with U.N. Member States—The United States may wish to continue to reach out to other U.N. member states to build consensus and form partnerships on reform policies, either within the framework of the United Nations or bilaterally. . . .U.S. support for certain U.N. reform initiatives can be a liability because some member states may view U.S. support as self-serving. In these cases, the United States may consider allowing like-minded countries [to] advocate its reform agenda.

Luisa Blanchfield,
Congressional Research Services,
December 15, 2009.

around the world where the Security Council has sent U.N. peacekeepers or where the U.N. has facilitated peace negotiations. Countries continue to wallow in poverty not because of a paucity of U.S. support for the U.N., but because of their own poor governance, corruption, and anti-market economic policies. The record of abuse, corruption, and mismanagement in U.N. institutions charged with delivering food, medicine, and other humanitarian assistance is unacceptable. Acknowledging these failings provides a much needed reality check between what the U.N. claims to do and what is actually being accomplished. The unintended consequences of failing to deal with the U.N. realistically lead to greater insecurity, poverty, and oppression.

As you have said, "The United States must champion reform so the United Nations can help us meet the challenges of the 21st century." But reforming the U.N. is not enough. The United States must continue to lead the international community in working through the U.N. when it can be effective, but it must also lead in establishing alternative mechanisms, coalitions, partnerships, alliances, and organizations when the U.N. proves to be lacking.

Confusion over Reform

To help make the reform that is desperately needed to ensure the U.N.'s effectiveness a reality, you and your Administration should:

Use America's financial leverage to focus the U.N. on key activities; trim outdated mandates and unnecessary expenses; and improve transparency, management, and accountability. In a July 2008 speech, you said, "It's time to reform the United Nations, so that this imperfect institution can become a more perfect forum to share burdens, strengthen our leverage, and promote our values." Regrettably, however, there is considerable confusion about the form that such reform should take.

Some countries see reform primarily as expansion of the U.N. Security Council on the premise that it no longer reflects the modern world, but any increase in membership would only exacerbate the council's tendency toward paralysis and inaction. For an Administration seeking to work closely with the U.N., expansion of the Security Council should be anathema [taboo].

Other countries see reform as expanding the U.N.'s power and authority by granting it regulatory authority over global issues like climate change and international financial transactions. But the well-publicized scandals involving the Iraq Oil-for-Food program, abuses by U.N. peacekeepers, recent revelations of corruption in U.N. procurement, and the U.N. Development Program's violation of its own rules and regulations in North Korea are evidence of deep-seated problems that must be addressed before the organization is given additional resources or authority.

The unfortunate reality is that most member states are not interested in dealing with the U.N.'s waste, inefficiency, mismanagement, lack of accountability, or opacity. The General Assembly agreed in the 2005 Outcome Document to adopt a number of reforms; but despite voluminous reports and proposals by former Secretary-General Kofi Annan and current Secretary-General Ban Ki-moon, it has failed to fully implement or enforce such measures as a review of U.N. mandates, enhanced oversight, and outsourcing to reduce costs.

America's Financial Leverage

In budget discussions this past fall [2008], a number of member states refused to continue to maintain the U.N. Procurement Task Force (PTF) as an independent investigatory entity, despite its success in uncovering hundreds of millions of dollars in fraud, waste, and mismanagement. Russia recently sought to prevent PTF staff from being transferred to the U.N.'s own investigatory unit, the Office of Internal Oversight Services.

History shows that the U.S., with only one vote out of 192 at the U.N., needs to use its financial leverage if it wishes to advance U.N. reform. Last year [2008], over objections by the United States, the U.N. passed the largest budget increase in its history while simultaneously failing to adopt key reforms, thereby breaking a 20-year tradition of consensus-based decisions on the budget. The decision to overrule the U.S.—which is by far the largest contributor to the U.N. regular budget— was met with a standing ovation by the other member states. Lacking a financial incentive, other nations felt little need to heed U.S. concerns on the budget.

U.S. interests are best advanced when policy decisions are based on a realistic appraisal of what works effectively and what does not. A number of U.N. technical agencies and specialized bodies and activities are effective and serve U.S. interests. They should be preserved. Others are hindered by policies, practices, and mandates that squander effort and resources. They should be reformed and refocused on their core missions. Finally, some parts or activities of the U.N. serve little practical function or are unable to fulfill their mandates and should be eliminated.

In other words, seeking to make the U.N. more effective and accountable requires that the U.S. focus its influence where it can be most effective and acknowledge where its efforts will be futile.

| "We stand at a true crossroads. We must move urgently to reinvigorate the basis for common action."

The United States Is Changing Its Approach to the United Nations

Susan Rice

The United States is becoming more supportive of the United Nations under the Barack Obama administration, Susan Rice asserts in the following viewpoint. She explains that the administration recognizes that it is facing challenges that require global cooperation and that the UN is indispensable at providing legitimacy for America's security interests. According to Rice, the United States is working with the UN in a number of ways to advance U.S. policies and universal rights, including participating constructively and meeting its financial obligations. Rice is the U.S. permanent representative to the United Nations.

As you read, consider the following questions:

1. What is the "fundamental imperative of U.S. national security in the 21st century," according to Rice?

Susan Rice, "A New Course in the World, a New Approach at the UN: Remarks at New York University's Center for Global Affairs and Center on International Cooperation," United States Mission to the United Nations, August 12, 2009.

2. As explained by Rice, on what country has the UN imposed the "toughest array of sanctions . . . in the world today"?

3. According to the author, how will the United States increase its support for UN peacekeeping efforts?

As the U.S. Ambassador to the United Nations, I'd like to offer some thoughts about how the United States is changing the course it charts in the world—and how, consistent with our new direction, we are rather dramatically changing our approach to the United Nations.

That change is essential because we face an extraordinary array of global challenges: poorly guarded nuclear weapons and material, a global financial meltdown, wars in Afghanistan and Iraq. Iran and North Korea building their nuclear weapons capabilities, al-Qaeda [terrorist group] and its affiliates, genocide and mass atrocities, cyber attacks on our digital infrastructure, international crime and drug trafficking, pandemics, and a climate that is warming by the day. These are transnational security threats that cross national borders as freely as a storm. By definition, they cannot be tackled by any one country alone.

Since taking office, the Obama Administration has acted internationally on the basis of three core premises. First, the global challenges we face cannot be met without U.S. leadership. But second, while U.S. leadership is necessary, it's rarely sufficient. We need the effective cooperation of a broad range of friends and partners. And third, others will likely shoulder a greater share of the global burden if the United States leads by example, acknowledges mistakes, corrects course when necessary, forges strategies in partnership and treats others with respect.

The reach, scale, and complexity of these 21st-century security challenges put unprecedented demands on states and the entire infrastructure of international cooperation that we helped to build after 1945. If ever there were a time for effective multilateral cooperation in pursuit of U.S. interests and a shared future of greater peace and prosperity, it is now. We stand at a true crossroads. We must move urgently to reinvigorate the basis for common action. The bedrock of that cooperation must be a community of states committed to solving collective problems and capable of meeting the responsibilities of effective sovereignty.

A fundamental imperative of U.S. national security in the 21st century is thus clear: we need to maximize the number of states with both the capacity and the will to tackle this new generation of transnational challenges. We need a modern edifice of cooperation, built upon the foundation of responsible American leadership, with the bricks of state capacity and the beams of political will. . . .

Our values compel us to reduce poverty, disease, and hunger, to end preventable deaths of mothers and children, and to build self-sufficiency in agriculture, health, and education. But so too does our national interest. Whether the peril is terrorism, pandemics, narcotics, human trafficking, or civil strife, a state so weak that it incubates a threat is also a state too weak to contain a threat.

In the 21st century, therefore we can have no doubt: as President Obama has said time and again, America's security and well-being are inextricably linked to those of people everywhere.

The UN Helps Rebuild Societies

Building the capacity of fragile states is a major part of our work every day at the United Nations, since it is the UN that is leading the charge in many of the toughest corners of the world. At its best, the UN helps rebuild shattered societies, lay the foundations of democracy and development, and establish conditions in which people can live in dignity and mutual respect. I have seen first-hand how the UN delivers—in Haiti, where peacekeepers flushed out deadly gangs from the notorious Cité Soleil slum and now are training a reformed Haitian police force. I have seen it in Liberia, where the UN Development Program supports impressive efforts to teach literacy, computer skills, and trade skills to jobless ex-combatants. I have seen it in Congo, where the UN has made it possible to hold the first democratic elections in that country's history.

It is not enough though simply to build up the corps of capable, democratic states. We need states with both the capacity and the will to tackle common challenges. As we have been reminded in recent years, we cannot take that will for granted, even among our closest allies. The simple reality is this: if we want others to help combat the threats that concern us most, then we must help others combat the challenges that threaten them most. For many nations, those threats are first and foremost the things that afflict human beings in their daily lives: corruption, repression, conflict, hunger, poverty, disease, and a lack of education and opportunity.

When the United States joins others to confront these challenges, it's not charity. It's not even barter. In today's world, more than ever, America's interests and values converge. What is good for others is often good for us. When we manifest our commitment to tackling the threats that menace so many other nations; when we invest in protecting the lives of others; and when we recognize that national security is no longer a zero-sum game, then we increase other countries' will to cooperate on the issues most vital to us.

We build that will by demonstrating responsible leadership. We build will by setting a tone of decency and mutual respect rather than condescension and contempt. We build will by abiding by the rules we expect others to follow. We build will by pursuing pragmatic, principled policies and explain[ing] them with intelligence and candor. And in the broadest sense, we build will when others can see their future as aligned with ours.

The UN Is Indispensable

All of this helps explain why so many of America's security interests come together today at the United Nations. Day in and day out, my colleagues and I at the U.S. Mission to the UN are working to build the will of countries to cooperate and to strengthen their means to act. We are actually on the front lines of what President Obama calls "a new era of engagement."

And that is why, I have to confess, it is actually a great time to be the U.S. Ambassador to the United Nations. Everyone notices when a superpower becomes an agent of change—in word and deed, in policy and tone. We are demonstrating that the United States is willing to listen, respect differences, and consider new ideas.

In both the Security Council and the General Assembly, we seek to forge common purpose with other nations. But the fact is: we cannot and will not always agree. Some things are not negotiable. We will always choose to stand firmly on principle rather than fade like cowards into a crowd.

And we have no illusions. A serious gap still separates the vision of the UN's founders from the institution of today. The Security Council is less riven than it was in the coldest days of the Cold War, but it still stumbles when interests and values diverge, as they do over such issues as Darfur, Zimbabwe, and Burma. In the General Assembly, member states still often let political theater distract from real deliberation and decision. Israel is still unfairly singled out. And the UN system still must confront waste and abuse even as it struggles to meet daunting new responsibilities for peacekeeping, humanitarian assistance, and development.

As President Obama has said, the UN is imperfect; but it is also indispensable. There can be no substitute for the legitimacy the UN can impart or its potential to mobilize the widest possible coalitions. There is no better alternative to sharing the costs and burdens of UN peace operations and humanitarian missions around the world. There is no doubt that we are more secure when the UN can foster nonproliferation and promote disarmament. It is we, along with others, who gain when the UN spurs sustainable development and democracy, improves global health, upholds women's rights, and broadens access to education. And we reap the benefits when the UN sets little-known global standards that enable our cell phones to work properly and our airplanes to fly more safely.

In short, the UN is essential to our efforts to galvanize concerted actions that make Americans safer and more secure.

Steering a New Course

Today, as we steer a new course at the United Nations, our guiding principles are clear: We value the UN as a vehicle for advancing U.S. policies and universal rights. We work for change from within rather than criticizing from the sidelines. We stand strong in defense of America's interests and values, but we don't dissent just to be contrary. We listen to states great and small. We build coalitions. We meet our responsibilities. We pay our bills. We push for real reform. And we remember that, in an interconnected world, what's good for others is often good for the United States as well.

Let me share with you six ways that we are putting these principles into practice every day.

First, we work at the UN to promote America's core security interests. Consider North Korea. We recently negotiated a unanimous Security Council resolution imposing the toughest array of sanctions on any country in the world today—including new asset freezes, sweeping financial sanctions, a complete embargo on arms exports, and an unprecedented set of obligations for the inspection of suspect vessels. These sanctions are aimed at pressing North Korea to fulfill its commitments and at achieving the complete, verifiable, and irreversible denuclearization of the Korean Peninsula.

We also continue to work in the Security Council to ensure that Iran meets its international obligations. . . .

The UN is also playing vital roles in two countries at the top of our national security agenda where American troops are in harm's way. In Iraq, the UN is providing expert advice on elections, mediating the longstanding internal boundary disputes between Arabs and Kurds, and assisting Iraqi citizens displaced by war.

In Afghanistan, the UN is helping to promote political development, coordinate donor assistance, support the August 20 elections, and build the capabilities of the Afghan state. All of this buttresses our comprehensive, new international strategy for Afghanistan.

And elsewhere, the UN strengthens America's security by preventing the smoldering embers of conflict from blazing back to life. For 60 years, the UN has played a crucial role in ending violent conflicts in such places as Korea, Namibia, Mozambique, Guatemala, Cyprus, the Golan Heights, Haiti, Liberia, and Sierra Leone. Where people are suffering—where conflict is enduring—where hope is fleeting—that is where you will find the United Nations.

Part of the Human Rights Council

Second, we participate constructively. Rather than throw up our hands, we roll up our sleeves to get things done.

Consider the UN Human Rights Council. Through three election cycles, the United States refused to seek a seat, dismissing the Council as flawed and anti-Israel—which obviously it is. But what did this approach achieve? Dictators were not called to account for their records of repression; abused citizens did not have their voices heard; obsessive, unproductive Israel-bashing raged on.

So in May [2009], we changed course and we won a seat on the Human Rights Council with 90 percent of the votes cast. We join this body well aware that, in many ways, the Human Rights Council is the poster child for what ails the UN. But sitting on the outside will not stop the posturing in Geneva nor defend those bleeding under the boot of despots.

Real change does not come from sitting on the sidelines. Real change can only come through painstaking, principled diplomacy. So we will work hard to reduce customary divisions. We will demand fair treatment for Israel. We will amplify the voices of those suffering under the world's cruelest regimes. And we will lead by example through our actions at home and our support for those risking their lives for democracy and human rights abroad.

It will not be easy. It will not be quick. But let's remember the words of a former university president who once said, "If you think education is expensive, try ignorance." Well, if you think engagement is imperfect, try isolation.

Third, we stand firm on principle and resolute on the issues that matter most—but we are resisting indulging in petty battles. In the past, we have sometimes let ourselves be defined by what we stand against, not what we stand for. Well no more. Over the past six months, the United States has taken a fresh look at our positions across the board— including some policies that left us and others scratching their heads to understand what we objected to—policies that failed to advance our interests or our values.

A New Direction

And that's why we have taken concrete steps in a new direction. We have changed course, embracing as our own the Millennium Development Goals, which the United States once shunned. We rescinded the Mexico City policy that barred U.S. assistance to programs that support family planning and reproductive health services. We stopped withholding U.S. contributions to the UN Population Fund. We signed the first new human rights convention of the 21st century, the UN Convention on the Rights of Persons with Disabilities. We reversed course to back a General Assembly resolution, excuse me, statement opposing violence and discrimination based on sexual orientation. We no longer oppose mentions of reproductive health or the International Criminal Court. We no longer balk at every reference to the "right to food" or the Convention on the Elimination of All Forms of Discrimination Against Women. And we're forging a new path on climate change commensurate with our global responsibilities.

These steps contribute to a world that is more prosperous, more peaceful, and more aligned with the universal values that this nation was founded upon. Through word and deed, the United States is showing that we are ready to lead once more.

Fourth, we seek constructive working relations with countries large and small. While we pursue more effective cooperation among the Security Council's five permanent members, we are also mindful of the fact that the Council has not just five members but 15, and that the UN has 192 in total. All of them vote in the General Assembly, and more than half of the UN's membership consists of small states with populations of less than 10 million people.

So we're reaching out not just to "the Permanent Five" and to our Western partners but to nations of all sizes in Africa, South and Southeast Asia, Latin America, the Caribbean, and the Pacific Islands—and to the dozens of Muslim-majority countries, many of whose Ambassadors gathered at my residence to watch President Obama's historic speech in Cairo.

We will work with the vast majority of countries on the basis of mutual interests and mutual respect and we will do so to bridge old divides, resisting the efforts of a handful to spoil shared progress. The rifts between North and South are almost as outdated as those between East and West. Yet there's still a widespread perception at the UN that the North cares only about security, and the South cares only about development. But such truisms ignore a central truth: there can be no security without development; and there can be no sustained development without security. These old-school rifts belie today's realities. Our fates are not opposed; they are intertwined.

And that makes engaging across the full UN membership much more than good manners. It's also smart diplomacy. So we invest in relationships, because in diplomacy, as in life, it can make the difference. . . .

Fifth, we meet our obligations. As we call upon others to help reform and strengthen the UN, the United States must do its part—and pay its bills. Our dues to the United Nations are treaty obligations, and we are committed to working with Congress to pay them in full and on time.

Thanks to strong support from Congress, we are now able to clear U.S. arrears to the UN's regular budget and to those on the peacekeeping budget, which accumulated between 2005 and 2008. And we will meet our 2009 peacekeeping obligations in full.

The Administration's Fiscal Year 2010 budget request, if fully funded by Congress, will keep us current on both our regular and peacekeeping accounts—and allow us to move toward ending the practice, started in the 1980s, of paying our bills to the UN and many other major international organizations nearly a year late. The United States cannot lead from a position of strength while we are awash in arrears. We cannot champion important UN missions in Iraq and Afghanistan and then turn around and oppose the budgets to fund them. So we will continue to work with Congress in a bipartisan spirit to meet our responsibilities.

And finally, we push for serious reform. All the world's citizens deserve a UN that runs right. So we are working to strengthen the UN's ability to deliver responsibly. It's not enough that costs be contained and funds spent without corruption; each dollar must serve its intended purpose, be it for development or peacekeeping. The UN needs greater efficiency and effectiveness.

Improving Peacekeeping Efforts

Central to our reform effort is our focus on the next generation of UN peacekeeping. UN missions have saved untold lives, averted numerous wars, and helped restore or establish democratic rule in more than a dozen countries. But the system is under severe strain. More than 115,000 military, police, and civilian peacekeepers are now deployed in 15 operations around the world—often in areas where there is hardly any peace to keep.

So we need mission mandates that are more credible and achievable. We need peacekeeping operations to be planned expertly, deployed quickly, budgeted realistically, equipped seriously, led ably, and ended responsibly. And we need to strengthen the security sector and the rule of law in such places as Liberia and Haiti so that peacekeepers can return home certain that their missions are truly accomplished.

We will increase U.S. support to UN peacekeeping— including by being willing to contribute more U.S. military staff officers, military observers, civilian police, and other civilian personnel to UN missions and by refocusing the U.S. Global Peace Operations Initiative on helping partner countries train their own peacekeepers. We are encouraging others to do more as well.

At the same time, we aim to ensure the UN has the management culture and leadership it needs to succeed. Our priorities are greater transparency and accountability, stronger ethics and oversight mechanisms, and buttressing Secretary-General Ban Ki-moon's initiatives to overhaul the UN's procurement and human resources practices.

Today's United Nations is a multi-billion-dollar enterprise facing greater demands than ever in more places than ever. As in any organization, there is no substitute for first-rate leadership. Both at UN Headquarters and in the field, far-sighted, hard-driving, broad-minded UN officials can make all the difference in the world. We want to work with others to continue to identify, promote, and empower. . . .

The UN Is Vital

I want to conclude by reinforcing a simple message: the United Nations is vital to our efforts to craft a better, safer world.

We have inherited a vast array of challenges. The world will no doubt hurl others at us. But we are not daunted. We are determined. We are advancing the vision, strategies, and programs that will renew America's leadership, strengthen our security, uphold our values, deepen our prosperity, and reinforce the alliances and partnerships that multiply our strength.

> "Governments, NGOs, the private sector, and international organizations such as the United Nations must work as partners to transform the role of women."

The United States Supports UN Goals Regarding Women

Meryl Frank

The United States is committed to working with the United Nations to improve the rights of women, Meryl Frank asserts in the following viewpoint taken from her speech to the UN Commission on the Status of Women. She argues that President Barack Obama's administration strongly supports women's economic and civil rights, but she adds that all member nations of the UN need to take action to end the mistreatment of women. Frank concludes that one way to improve the condition of women worldwide is by successfully responding to the HIV/AIDS crisis. Frank is the U.S. representative to the UN Commission on the Status of Women.

As you read, consider the following questions:

1. What is the Mexico City Policy, as defined by Frank?

Meryl Frank, "Statement: The Equal Sharing of Responsibilities Between Women and Men, Including Caregiving in the Context of HIV/AIDS," Commission of the Status of Women, March 4, 2009. Reproduced by permission of the author.

2. According to the author, what are the five strategies of the President's Emergency Plan for AIDS Relief (PEPFAR)?

3. How many children have been born HIV-free due to PEPFAR, as stated by Frank?

Let there be no doubt: The United States is firmly committed to promoting women's empowerment and well-being, both at home and around the world. We see this gathering as an important forum for renewing our efforts. This group represents women and men worldwide who are striving for women's equality and empowerment. These are global aims, and your creativity, energy, and intellect are huge assets to our common efforts. The entire U.S. delegation looks forward to working closely with our fellow delegates and with the hundreds of representatives from women's organizations and other civil society groups.

The United States is determined to help ensure that women and girls have not just full civil rights, but also the education, the nutrition, the medical care, and the economic opportunities that they need and deserve. President Obama has already shown that he is a strong advocate for women's issues. As one of his first acts, President Obama repealed the so-called Mexico City Policy, which prohibited NGOs [nongovernmental organizations] working abroad from using U.S. funding to provide—or even offer counseling about—the full range of family planning options. By moving swiftly, President Obama has empowered women to gain access to the health information and services they need to maintain their own well-being and the health of their families. To further improve women's health, global development, and family planning, the Administration looks forward to working with Congress to restore U.S. financial support for the U.N. Population Fund.

Protecting Women in Wartime

[The UN Security Council]: *Calls on* all parties to armed conflict to take special measures to protect women and girls from gender-based violence, particularly rape and other forms of sexual abuse, and all other forms of violence in situations of armed conflict;

Emphasizes the responsibility of all States to put an end to impunity and to prosecute those responsible for genocide, crimes against humanity, and war crimes including those relating to sexual and other violence against women and girls.

UN Security Council, Resolution 1325, October 31, 2000.

In addition, President Obama has signed legislation that finally protects women in the United States from salary discrimination.

The President has appointed other strong leaders on these issues. As you well know, Secretary of State Hillary Clinton led the U.S. delegation to the historic Beijing Women's Conference in 1995. As Secretary of State, she will, of course, be an eloquent advocate for women's rights worldwide.

We are fortunate to have another strong leader on women's issues in Susan Rice, the U.S. ambassador to the UN. In her confirmation hearings, Ambassador Rice spoke in favor of ratifying the Convention on the Elimination of Discrimination Against Women. She strongly said that it is "past time" to get this done, and doing so "will be an important priority for this Administration."

Treaties Alone Will Not Suffice

As the United States continues to bring new energy to these issues, it will review the binding global pacts that help empower women. That includes the Convention on the Rights of Persons with Disabilities and the Convention on the Rights of the Child. We will remain committed to working with the international community to promote many of the principles embodied in these conventions.

But as you know, signing treaties or announcing a clear international standard is not enough to improve the lives of millions of women. As Secretary Clinton said during her recent trip to Asia, "It is important to raise the role of women on an ongoing basis. All women should exercise their rights to be fully functioning, productive citizens." In order to do so, governments, NGOs, the private sector, and international organizations such as the United Nations must work as partners to transform the role of women in their societies. The United States urges member states to fully implement Security Council Resolution 1325 on women, peace, and security, and Security Council Resolution 1820 on sexual violence against women in conflict situations. We need urgent action in the fight to end violence against women, honor crimes [killing of women in order to preserve family honor], commercial sexual exploitation, and trafficking in persons.

We must also work to support women's and men's efforts to balance work and family. In our own country, we can do better at providing quality child-care, elder care, and flexible work hours, and we can do more to address the concerns of the many American women who work full-time but feel as if they are not meeting either their responsibilities at home or their responsibilities in the workplace. We can also do more to encourage men's participation in family care.

Let me offer a personal aside here. While working at the World Health Organization (WHO) in Copenhagen, Denmark on the International Code of the Marketing of Breast Milk Substitutes, I first recognized that working women should be able to take a period of leave following the birth of a child without losing their jobs or benefits. However, the United

States at that time was one of the few nations that offered no maternal or parental leave policy at the national level. I was proud to be an author of the national Family and Medical Leave Act that provides eligible employees with a leave from work to recover from a serious illness or to care for a new-born, newly adopted or seriously ill child, parent, or spouse. Care-giving is something that I know about and care about, and I can assure you that the Administration cares about it too. . . .

The Challenge of HIV/AIDS

Men and women share important duties when it comes to care-giving, and this is especially true with HIV/AIDS. HIV/AIDS poses a unique challenge to the health and development of women and girls worldwide. The U.S. is responding through the President's Emergency Plan for AIDS Relief, or PEPFAR, as well as by supporting the Global Fund to Fight HIV/AIDS, Tuberculosis, and Malaria. Gender issues are incorporated into all aspects of PEPFAR's prevention, care, and treatment programs, with a commitment to five strategies:

- Increasing gender equity in HIV/AIDS-related activities and services.

- Addressing male norms and behaviors that may worsen the epidemic.

- Reducing violence and coercion against women.

- Increasing women's access to income and productive resources.

- And deepening women's legal rights and protection.

PEPFAR has been a remarkable success story in its first five years. A key reason has been our commitment to incorporating gender awareness into its programs, including acknowledging the pivotal role of men. Thus far, the United States has:

- Helped provide treatment for 2.1 million people;

- Helped care for more than 10 million people living with HIV/AIDS, of which more than 40% are orphans and vulnerable children; and

- PEPFAR has helped prevent mother-to-child transmission of HIV during nearly 16 million pregnancies, thereby leading to nearly 240,000 children to be born HIV-free, who would otherwise be born HIV-positive. . . .

We have taken important steps, but there is much more to be done. The United States is fully dedicated to advancing the rights of women. Equality for women across all levels of society is vital to global progress, and today it is vital to rebuilding our global economy.

On behalf of the United States, I assure you that the U.S. delegation is eager to meet with you, to work with you, to exchange ideas with you, and to strive with you, so that together we can craft a world in which women and men can achieve their potential and enjoy full and complete lives.

Periodical Bibliography

The following articles have been selected to supplement the diverse views presented in this chapter.

Michael P. Farris   "New World Playpen," *American Conservative*, September 2009.

Andrew Ferguson   "Passive-Aggressive at the U.N.," *Weekly Standard*, October 5, 2009.

Edward Bernard Glick   "The US Should Leave the UN," *Portland Oregonian*, December 28, 2009.

Mark Leon Goldberg   "The Arsonist," *American Prospect*, January 2006.

Neil Macfarquhar   "A U.S. Envoy with a Case for Why the U.N. Matters," *New York Times*, September 22, 2009.

Susan E. Rice,   "Ambassador to the World," *Newsweek
interviewed by   International*, July 27, 2009.
*Newsweek
International*

Brett Schaefer and   "Malloch Brown Is Wrong: The U.S. Should
Nile Gardiner   Press Even Harder for UN Reform," *Human Events*, June 19, 2006.

Stephen Schlesinger   "A New Administration and the UN," *World Policy Journal*, Winter 2008.

Stephen Schlesinger   "Bosom Buddies? Ban and Obama's Curious Relations," *World Policy Journal*, Spring 2010.

Ian Williams   "Concern for U.N. 'Reform' Often Stops Short of Enforcing Resolutions," *Washington Report on Middle East Affairs*, May-June 2006.

CHAPTER 4

What Is the Future of the United Nations?

Chapter Preface

Reforming the United Nations is an idea that has been debated frequently. One idea that has gained popularity in recent years is to replace the UN with a new organization, the League of Democracies. The idea behind the League of Democracies is that it would be an organization where the United States and like-minded nations could work together on international issues without having to work within the UN system and its nondemocratic members.

Supporters of the league argue that a League of Democracies is an essential replacement, or at least supplement, to the UN because powerful nations such as China and Russia often veto actions that would benefit Western interests. In particular, advocates contend, autocracies frequently prevent the UN from taking action on human rights issues. As Jonah Goldberg writes in *National Review*: "I think a League of Democracies, in some form, is inevitable if for no other reason than that we'll have little choice but to find new strategic tools. China, Russia, and much of the Muslim world see the U.N. chiefly as a means of tripping up the U.S. Eventually, we're going to need to look elsewhere, and that's going to be to our friends—who are democracies."

However, not all critics of the UN believe a new organization should replace it in the future. Instead, they contend that the United States and other democracies should in fact spend more time collaborating with autocracies. Charles A. Kupchan, writing for *Foreign Affairs*, asserts: "Such a club . . . would draw new lines between democracies and nondemocracies." Kupchan and other opponents of a League of Democracies point out that the world's democracies already collaborate on a regular basis and do not need a formalized organization; furthermore, there already are organizations such as the North Atlantic Treaty Organization (NATO) that fulfill many of the aims of such a league.

The future of the United Nations could take many forms. The organization could undergo piecemeal reform, be overhauled entirely, or remain essentially unchanged. The authors in this chapter offer their own ideas, opinion, and forecasts on the issue.

| *"The United Nations . . . needs a funda-
mental structural reorganization."*

The UN Security Council and General Assembly Need Reforming

Rodrigue Tremblay

*Rodrigue Tremblay contends in the following viewpoint that the
United Nations must reorganize in order to achieve its goals. According to Tremblay, this reform should include an expansion of
the Security Council and an end to the veto power of its five primary members. He also argues that reforming the General Assembly by requiring a three-quarters majority vote for major decisions would ensure that the United Nations avoids division
between large and small nations. Tremblay is a professor emeri-
tus of economics at the University of Montreal.*

As you read, consider the following questions:

1. According to Tremblay, what was the original role of the
   United Nations?

Rodrigue Tremblay, "Mr. Ban Ki-Moon and the Future of the United Nations," *Global
Research*, Center for Research on Globalization, January 13, 2008. Reproduced by permission.

2. Which four nations does the author believe should join the current five permanent members of the Security Council?

3. What possible reform does Tremblay suggest could raise the democratic profile of the General Assembly?

A new Secretary-General has presided over the United Nations for more than a year, but most people ignore this fact. They can be forgiven, because very little has resulted from the October 13, 2006 election by the 192-member United Nations General Assembly of a shy South Korean diplomat, Mr. Ban Ki-Moon, as the U.N. Secretary-General. On January 1, 2007, Mr. Ban Ki-moon took office as the eighth U.N. Secretary-General, succeeding Mr. Kofi Annan, for a first term lasting until December 31, 2011. He was a compromise candidate among seven candidates for the post, and he succeeded in avoiding a veto from any of the five permanent members of the Security Council. He was particularly popular with the [George W.] Bush-[Dick] Cheney administration because, in his capacity of Minister of Foreign Affairs and Trade, he had pushed his own government to send South Korean troops to Iraq.

We should recall that one of the first moves by Mr. Ban Ki-moon, soon after he took office, was to reverse a long-standing United Nations opposition to the death penalty as a human rights concern. Indeed, he condoned the death penalty that had been handed down on the deposed Iraqi President Saddam Hussein by the Iraqi High Tribunal, stating, "The issue of capital punishment is for each and every member State to decide."

Mr. Ban Ki-moon has also been criticized for appointing a large number of his fellow South Korean nationals to key U.N. posts, and for showing nepotism in appointing his own son-in-law to a key United Nations post in Iraq.

Minor Reforms Instituted

It remains to be seen if Mr. Ban Ki-moon has the vision, the credibility and the moral authority to bring forward the reforms that the United Nations urgently needs, if it is going to avoid the fate of irrelevancy that beset the League of Nations. So far, the only reforms the new Secretary-General has espoused have been minor administrative arrangements—and even those were contested—such as splitting the U.N. peacekeeping operation into one department handling operations and another handling arms. His proposal to combine the political affairs and disarmament department was even rejected outright.

What the United Nations needs is more than simply shuffling the chairs on the deck of the Titanic [i.e., making small changes in the face of a looming disaster]. It needs a fundamental structural reorganization if it is to play the role it was assigned originally in 1945; that is to say, to promote international cooperation and to maintain international peace and security. This overall goal can only be achieved if the United Nations has the legitimacy and the means to prevent wars and to promote human rights throughout the world.

But, what should the Secretary-General, with the support of member states, do? Logically, Mr. Ban Ki-moon should begin by declaring that the post–World War II [WWII] era is over and that the main obstacle to any substantial reform of the U.N. should be removed. There is, indeed, a relic of the Second World War which is still in place. It is the veto power that the five winning nations (USA, Russia, China, U.K. and France) gave themselves after WWII in the functioning of the U.N. Security Council. Mr. Ban Ki-moon should plead with the five above[-mentioned] countries to show magnanimity and, while retaining their permanent status at the Security Council as an historical given, convince them that they should voluntarily forgo the antiquated veto that paralyses any attempt at reforming the United Nations and at making it a functional organization. Presently, because of the veto feature, each time one of the five permanent member states is involved in a crisis or in an international dispute, the Security Council and the entire United Nations are paralyzed.

The Secretary-General should tackle the task of improving the U.N.'s democratic legitimacy and operational efficiency through fundamental reforms of the Security Council and the General Assembly. Both bodies are antiquated and ill adapted to fulfill their tasks.

Reforming the Security Council

First, in a true 21st century spirit, the United Nations Security Council (UNSC) should better reflect the new demographic, political, and economic realities that have emerged over the last sixty years. There is a wide consensus that political and economic powerhouses such as Japan, India, Brazil and Germany, the G4 nations, should join the current five permanent members in the Security Council. These countries are large and stable democracies and economic giants that should not be left out of the world decision process.

With the current ten countries that join the Council on a regional basis, in a rotating system, for two-years terms, after having been elected by the General Assembly, a new 19-member Security Council would remain small enough to be efficient. As a substitute to the present veto enjoyed by a few members, a three-quarters majority rule could be implemented in order to guarantee that the Council's decisions reflect at all times a worldwide consensus. This would mean that the decisions and measures, couched in the form of resolutions, and which are arrived at by the Council, would have to be supported by at least fifteen members. Since all Members of the United Nations agree to accept and carry out the decisions of the Security Council, under the U.N. Charter, such a requirement would seem to be necessary if the U.N. actions are to carry a wide acceptance.

One big obstacle to enlarging the Security Council comes from the insistence of some African countries to have a permanent representative of their continent on the Council. While this is a most legitimate claim in principle, it is a difficult one to achieve in practice. First, there is no consensus in Africa about which candidate among three possible candidates (Egypt, Nigeria or South Africa) should be elected. And second, even among the latter, none seems to meet the requirements of long-term political stability and economic dynamism and leadership that one would expect from a permanent member. It would be most unfortunate if the movement to reform the U.N. were to be paralyzed because of these facts.

Presently, the presidency of the Security Council rotates among the members of the Council monthly, in alphabetical order. This leaves the U.N. Secretary-General somewhat out of the loop, even though he should be seen as the main spokesperson for the United Nations. An obvious reform would be to designate the Secretary-General as the ex-officio presiding officer of the Council. He would then cease to be regarded as simply a dignified bureaucrat who heads the U.N. Secretariat, rather than being the main spokesperson for the whole United Nations.

Democratizing the General Assembly

While it is true that the U.N. is not a world government, but rather a forum for the world's 192 sovereign states to debate issues and determine collective courses of action, this does not mean that it should not improve its democratic legitimacy, especially as the world has become more and more globalized and is in need of new institutions to reflect this new reality.

Presently the General Assembly is composed of all member nations, and each one of them has an equal number of representatives designated by their respective governments. This world parliament, which meets annually from September to December, has important responsibilities, such as to oversee

the budget of the U.N., appoint the non-permanent members to the Security Council, and receive reports from other bodies of the U.N.—such important issues have to be decided by a two-thirds majority of those members present and voting. The General Assembly can also adopt resolutions on other subjects and this then only requires a simple majority. Each member country has one vote. On the other hand, such resolutions are not binding on the member states and the Security Council has no obligation to implement them, with the consequence that in most cases, they remain pious wishes. We can therefore say that the General Assembly de facto functions as a limited world parliament, but only for governments.

A possible reform designed to raise the democratic profile and prestige of the General Assembly among people world-wide would be to assign four representatives to each member country and to encourage countries to have half of them, or better still, all of them, elected in country-wide general elections. This could be the most important step to ensure that the United Nations be seen as a truly representative international body.

On the other hand, since there is no proportional representation in the U.N., and to ensure that its decisions are made and supported by a large worldwide consensus, and especially to avoid a potentially disastrous structural North-South split, a three-quarters majority or even an eighty-percent decision rule could be mandated for important decisions. Presently, because of the one state, one vote system, it is theoretically possible for small states comprising just eight percent of the world population to pass a resolution by a two-thirds vote. No large country would ever accept to place its fate and interests in the hands of such a small group of people.

This, of course, is an incomplete list of issues and ideas about how to proceed to reform the United Nations.

| *"Any reform of the Security Council will be impossible for a long time."*

Reform of the UN Security Council Is Unlikely

Sven Bernhard Gareis and Johannes Varwick

In the following viewpoint Sven Bernhard Gareis and Johannes Varwick argue that reform of the United Nations Security Council is doubtful because of difficult-to-resolve questions over which countries should become members and whether the right of veto should remain. They contend that reform and expansion of the council is necessary because the world has changed significantly since the UN was founded, but opine that even a compromise solution, such as expanding the council to twenty-four members, is unlikely to be adopted in the foreseeable future. Gareis is a research director at the Bundeswehr Institute of Social Sciences, Hamburg, Germany, and Varwick is a professor of political sciences at the University of Kiel, Institute of Security Policy, Kiel, Germany.

Sven Bernhard Gareis and Johannes Varwick, *The United Nations: An Introduction.* Basingstoke, Hampshire: Palgrave Macmillan, 2005. Original German language edition copyright © Leske & Budrich, 2003. Translation and new, revised matter copyright © Sven Bernhard Gareis and Johannes Varwick, 2005. All rights reserved. Reproduced with permission of Palgrave Macmillan.

As you read, consider the following questions:

1. What change to the Security Council occurred in 1971, as explained by the authors?

2. In the authors' view, what is the first unanswered question that is keeping reforms from occurring?

3. According to Gareis and Varwick, why did NATO bypass the Security Council during the Kosovo crisis?

The modernization of the most important main body of the UN constitutes one of the organization's greatest challenges, and is thus also a decisive test of its capacity for comprehensive reform of any kind. In this task, all the difficulties and obstacles of institutional remodelling are collected together in microcosm. Article 23 of the [UN] Charter states that the Security Council shall consist of five (specifically named) permanent members and ten non-permanent members chosen according to the principle of equitable geographical distribution. The non-permanent members are chosen by the General Assembly for a term of two years, and may not serve two consecutive terms. This article was changed once in 1963, when the 28th General Assembly recommended that the number of non-permanent members be raised from six to ten. The Article 108 amendment process took a surprisingly short two years, and the change came into effect in 1965. With this change, the UN indicated that the size and composition of the Security Council should keep pace, at least to some extent, with the increasing total membership of the organization. Whereas in 1965 this number stood at 115, it had grown to 191 by 2004, and there have been constant initiatives since the 1970s to further increase the numbers of non-permanent members. Such efforts have continued to be sidelined.

With regard to the permanent members, there have been two changes. In 1971, the People's Republic of China replaced the Republic of China (Taiwan) both as a member of the UN and in the permanent seat on the Security Council. In December 1991, the permanent representative of the Russian Federation communicated to the Secretary-General that his country would be replacing the dissolved Soviet Union in the General Assembly and the Security Council. Although the Soviet Union is named specifically in Article 23 as a permanent member, both the General Assembly and the other permanent members accepted this simplified rule of succession without changing the Charter.

A New Global Order

Furthermore, with the renewed effectiveness of the Security Council in the post–Cold War era, energetic noises came both from important financial contributors (such as Japan and Germany) as well as the Non-Aligned Movement, that the Security Council's composition, decisional mechanisms and operating procedures (which had remained unchanged since the provisional rules of procedure from 1946), should be altered. In contrast to earlier initiatives, these attempts aimed not only at the addition of more non-permanent members, but also at changes to the permanent members' circle. The privileges that the permanent members enjoy through their permanent representation and veto right are no longer considered appropriate to the times. As understandable and sensible as this elevated position for a few states may have been in the year 1945 and during the Cold War, the constellation seems less appropriate half a century later. The massive developments of the last few decades, the end of the Cold War, the process of decolonization and the appearance of new states, have created a new global order to which the power distribution in the Security Council no longer corresponds. New political groupings have emerged, and new forms and centres of conflict have arisen. Africa and Latin America, however, continue to lack any representation among the permanent members, and the entire Asiatic region is represented by only one country—the People's Republic of China.

An Exercise in Futility

Security Council expansion is the briar patch of global governance reform. Fifteen years of failed efforts to add permanent members to the council have produced a hardened sense among UN experts that reform is an exercise in futility. Expanding the council was a centerpiece of [former UN Secretary-General] Kofi Annan's reform effort; the effort not only failed, but came close to dragging down the rest of the reform program with it. Current members of the "P-5" [five permanent members] do not wish to see their power diluted through the addition of new permanent members, even if the newcomers would not command the same right of veto as the current members.

James Traub, Stanley Foundation,
June 2009. www.stanleyfoundation.org.

At the 47th General Assembly, India proposed a resolution for the reform of the Security Council, which the General Assembly passed in November 1992. In it, it was determined that the 48th General Assembly should concern itself with a comprehensive discussion of this issue. The Secretary-General was given the task of requesting written statements from the member states to serve as a starting-point for the debate. Initially, in the summer of 1993, there were fifty more-or-less constructive suggestions for the future size and composition, decision-making structures and operational procedures of the Council. Eventually, the number of suggestions grew to 140. Following a rather short first discussion, in the autumn of 1993 the General Assembly delegated the negotiation of proposals as well as the further reform work to a working group created specifically for the purpose and open to all member states.

The Most Realistic Proposal

The very diverse proposals coming from the member states cannot possibly be addressed in full here. Neither can the working group's reports, which essentially communicate the general helplessness to be expected from a situation where all possible arguments are put forward, but no decisions can be made. Instead, we shall attempt to sketch out the lines along which some compromise appears possible, and to discuss the most prominent obstacles. This discussion will be based on a proposal made by the President of the 51st General Assembly, Razali Ismail from Malaysia, on 20 March 1997 in his function as the president of the working group. His initiative was planned to be included in December 1997 in a framework resolution of the General Assembly on Security Council reform, but this was prevented by a small group of states under Italy's leadership. In spite of its initial failure, this proposal can still be regarded as the basic model for Security Council reform most likely to meet with real success.

According to this suggestion, the Council should be expanded by a further five permanent and four non-permanent members, to reach a total strength of twenty-four. The new permanent members should include two industrialized states as well as one representative of the developing countries from each of the African, Asian and Latin American-Caribbean regions. The four new non-permanent member seats should be dedicated to one African, one Asian, one Latin-Caribbean and one Eastern European state. The five new permanent members should be chosen together, in order to avoid a so-called quick fix—that is, the rapid inclusion of a smaller number of new permanent members. With respect to the veto, it was suggested that the new permanent members should not enjoy that right, and that the original permanent five should begin to use it less and less frequently. Razali Ismail's idea accords with the state of the discussion both in the UN bodies and among the member states themselves. With respect to increasing the number of non-permanent members, the USA has in the meantime given up its objection that an overly-large Council will be incapable of making any decisions at all.

On the veto issue, the proposal makes concessions to the current political and legal realities. The provisions of Article 27 that form the basis for the veto can be changed only by changing the Charter, which would require the ratification of all five permanent members. It can hardly be expected that the permanent five will willingly give up their most important privilege. It is equally not to be expected that they will want to share this right with other states. Furthermore, the admission of even more veto players into the Security Council would make the already difficult process of interest-balancing into one of practical impossibility. On the other hand, the creation of a third member category of permanent members without a veto would also lead to status and prestige problems, which could have negative effects on the Council's work. If the ideal solution of a complete abolition of the individual veto and the introduction of a quorum that would make it impossible for a substantial minority to be outvoted by the majority simply cannot be achieved, then the 'second-best' Razali solution should be given preference over the status quo.

Two Major Issues Remain

There is widespread belief in the necessity for reform, and there has been a great deal of convergence in various state positions in recent years. Nevertheless, the realization of most of these reforms is still nowhere in sight. This is primarily because of two still-unanswered questions. First, there has been no agreement on which states should become the new permanent members. While Japan seems to be widely accepted as the choice for the Asian group, a number of nations from the Western European and Other States group, under the leadership of Italy, have set themselves against a permanent seat for Germany. They fear a relative weakening of their own influence in Europe as well as in international politics if Germany is allowed entry to the exclusive club. The situation in the other three state groups remains thoroughly unclear. The further permanent seat for Asia is being fought over energetically by India, Pakistan and Indonesia, while Brazil, Argentina and Mexico tussle over the seat for Latin America. In Africa, the ambitions of Egypt, Nigeria and South Africa must all be taken into account. Because, on purely domestic political grounds, none of these states can afford to give up its struggle for a permanent seat, no end to this discussion is in sight. Germany's suggestion of rotating several countries from a particular region through a permanent seat could conceivably be accepted by the African, Asian and Latin-American countries only if the two seats for industrialized countries were also subjected to the rotation principle. However, when states that co-operate as closely with one another as those in the EU [European Union] cannot agree on a rotation principle because of divergent interests and status, it is hardly likely that other state groups will manage it.

The second, and perhaps even more serious problem, is that of the veto. The 1997 line of compromise, first to have a two-step process of expansion and then further discussion of a modification or abolition of the right of veto, appears to have been destroyed by the 'all-or-nothing' position taken by the developing countries. Their stance is understandable when one considers that the point of reform is to deconstruct current forms of discrimination. On the other hand, two-step reform can be seen as the lesser of two evils when it is compared to the status quo in which only the permanent five have the privilege of both permanent representation and veto.

Reform of the Security Council remains vital for the continued acceptance of its authority and the legitimacy of its decisions. This was shown by the Kosovo crisis in 1998–9, when the blockade of the Security Council by the threats of Russian and Chinese vetoes led NATO [North Atlantic Treaty Organization] to simply bypass the Council altogether and take military action. The Iraq dispute of 2002–3 underscored this necessity once again. In a rule-based system of international politics, and above all in a collective security system, in which states make decisions with far-reaching consequences and existential significance for other countries, it is essential that the exercise of power be limited and brought under control. Even without a right of veto, states with permanent representation on the Security Council can exercise more influence over decisions than non-permanent members, and contribute to a broader basis of acceptance for such decisions. Even the possibilities of encouraging the current permanent five to limit their use of the veto voluntarily would be more nuanced and realistic coming from a permanent member than from any other member state. However, the fear remains that in the wake of the Iraq debate, any reform of the Security Council will be impossible for a long time. While the right of veto once more demonstrated its problematic side, the five holders of it will now cling to it even more insistently. Hopes that the USA might contribute to a strengthening of the Security Council through active co-operation in reform now seem completely illusory. Reform of the Security Council must be considered postponed until further notice.

"*The UN cannot act effectively if . . . major powers like the United States, Russia, China and other regional powers, do not support UN actions.*"

The World's Powers Must Support the United Nations

Shoji Ogawa

In the following viewpoint, Shoji Ogawa asserts that the United Nations needs international support—in particular, support from the United States and Japan—if it is to be effective. According to Ogawa, the UN cannot maintain peacekeeping operations or end hostilities around the world if the world's most powerful nations do not recognize that the UN can provide international legitimacy. According to Ogawa, the United States and Japan are vital to making the UN more effective because they are the two largest contributors to the organization. Ogawa is the consul general of Japan in Atlanta, Georgia.

As you read, consider the following questions:

1. In Ogawa's view, why is it unfair to accuse the UN when it cannot act effectively in certain crises?

Shoji Ogawa, "The UN: What It Can and Can't Do, and How the United States and Japan Can Make It More Effective," *American Diplomacy*, February 5, 2008. Reproduced by permission of the author.

2. How much of an expansion of the UN Security Council would the United States accept, according to the author?

3. Why does Ogawa believe it is worth the effort for the United States to go through the UN before taking military action?

I spent many years of my career working on UN affairs, and through those experiences, I have come to believe that the UN deserves our strong support in order to secure a better and safer world. I served three assignment tours at the Japanese mission to the United Nations in New York, representing the Japanese government. During these three periods, I covered various fields, such as international economic problems, including development, political affairs, and administrative and budgetary affairs. My work as a diplomat at the UN was an exciting experience. At the United Nations, you work with representatives from nearly all the countries of the world. The issues dealt with are incredibly diverse, ranging from the very technical to broad political matters.

UN Often Misunderstood

A well known former American Ambassador to the UN once made a famous remark: "If the UN Secretariat building in New York lost 10 stories, it wouldn't make a bit of difference." Of course, he said he was just joking, but it reveals a negative image or deep-rooted apathy that certain American officials and politicians hold for the UN. It is sometimes fashionable to bash the UN for its failure to act effectively or label it as biased in matters such as the Palestine-Israeli conflict or human rights violations by certain member states.

I regret that the United Nations and its activities are often misunderstood or not accurately known, which may lead to unrealistically high expectations or unwarranted accusations of incompetence. I believe that it is very important for Americans to form balanced opinions on the United Nations and its activities, because U.S. policy toward the UN is of critical importance to the success or failure of its activities. . . .

The UN Is a Melting Pot

Today, I will address three main questions: First, what is the UN? Second, what can the UN do, and what can't the UN do? And third, how can the United States and Japan make the UN effective and useful for us and for the world? I will do my best to make these points not by describing generalities but by illustrating specific activities and through my own experiences at the world body.

Every year, during two weeks in the middle of September the traffic in New York City becomes impossible. World leaders, heads of state, presidents, prime ministers and foreign ministers come to attend the United Nations General Assembly to deliver their policy speeches. They gather not only to deliver speeches, but also to take advantage of this occasion to meet other leaders bilaterally and in groups. These meetings take place at the delegate lounges in the UN building, in the offices of various countries' missions, and in the hotels where these leaders stay. They move around Manhattan from one place to another with Secret Service bodyguards in motorcades, making the already bad Manhattan traffic hopeless.

One particular memory I have from working as a junior Japanese delegate at the UN during the General Assembly is sitting and waiting with a few of my colleagues on delegate lounge sofas, in order to secure a place for our prime minister or foreign minister to meet with the ministers from other countries. It was not a very pleasant job. When I walked through the lounge, I saw many people that one usually only sees in newspapers and on television, like Cuban President Fidel Castro, then-PLO [Palestine Liberation Organization] chairman [Yasser] Arafat, and other well known figures passing by or having talks here and there. It was a fascinating scene.

Top 10 Donators to the UN Budget, 2009	
Member state	**Contribution (% of UN budget)**
United States	22.000%
Japan	16.624%
Germany	8.577%
United Kingdom	6.642%
France	6.301%
Italy	5.079%
Canada	2.977%
Spain	2.968%
China	2.667%
Mexico	2.257%
Other member states	23.908%

TAKEN FROM: http://www.un.org.

What I would like to convey through these memories is that the UN is a huge debating club, a melting pot of various perspectives, where world opinions are forged through meetings, debates, and negotiations. At present, the UN is the most universal international organization, represented by 192 of the world's countries. It provides an indispensable forum to discuss all kinds of international issues.

The UN Needs Support

The UN is often attacked with claims, particularly by the United States, that it is unduly biased in certain matters such as the Arab-Israeli conflict and human rights issues. This is due to the fact that many members of the UN are countries with sympathetic positions toward Arab states or countries without democratic systems of governance. It is not the fault of the UN, but the reality of the present world.

The UN is not a super-national body, as may be misunderstood by many people and even by some politicians. The policies and actions of the UN are decided through agreements by member states, not by the international bureaucrats working for the UN Secretariat. The Secretariat is merely an executive body to implement the policies and activities dictated by the member states.

Therefore, the UN cannot act effectively if member states, particularly major powers like the United States, Russia, China and other regional powers, do not support UN actions. That's why the Security Council, the most important and powerful organ of the UN, has five permanent members with veto power.

This leads to my second point: What the UN can and cannot do. When I was serving as the Japanese delegate in charge of political affairs at the Japanese Mission to the UN, most recently from 1994 to 1997, the most pressing issue was the conflict in the former Yugoslavian Republic of Bosnia Herzegovina. The UN peacekeeping forces that were deployed to protect Muslim inhabitants did not have sufficient military capability nor authority to respond to attacks from Serbian forces, because Russia, favoring the Serbian faction, did not support giving a strong mandate to UN forces. Also, the Western powers including the United States were reluctant to directly intervene in the conflict.

Consequently, UN forces suffered humiliating capitulation to Serbian attacks and remained powerless before the ethnic cleansing perpetrated by the Serbs. The situation improved and peace was finally achieved when the United States intervened and negotiations between warring factions produced an agreement in Dayton, Ohio. The peacekeeping responsibility was assigned to NATO [North Atlantic Treaty Organization], replacing UN peacekeeping forces.

The UN Reflects International Politics

On the other hand, the Lebanon crisis that arose as a result of Israel's attack and invasion in the summer of 2006 was effectively dealt with in the context of the UN, as major powers supported sending UN peacekeeping forces into southern Lebanon to monitor compliance with the Security Council resolution calling for Israeli withdrawal and the cessation of hostilities by [Islamist organization] Hezbollah forces. In this case, even Israel, which regards the UN as biased against it, admitted the usefulness of the UN's role in maintaining the stability of the border with Lebanon, and agreed to the deployment of UN forces in southern Lebanon. From these examples, we can say that the UN is a reflection of the realities of international politics. Nothing more, nothing less. Therefore, it is unfair to accuse the UN when it cannot act effectively as in the cases of Bosnia Herzegovina, the Rwandan massacre, or Darfur, because in each of these situations, there was no strong support by major powers to act quickly and effectively.

However, when agreement does exist among major powers, as in the case of Lebanon or North Korea's missile and nuclear testing, the UN is a useful instrument to advance the cause of international peace and security by providing an effective means of implementing agreements or exerting political pressure on the international community.

We are faced with many issues that require global cooperation and actions. The most prominent issues among them are: climate change, the fight against international terrorism, and the proliferation of weapons of mass destruction. The UN and its affiliated international agencies and organizations are an indispensable forum to discuss, negotiate, and implement joint policies to address those issues.

Important Roles

The United States and Japan can and should take initiative with all those issues through the context of the UN. With regard to the issue of climate change, the process for negotiating a post-Kyoto Protocol framework started with the COP 13 conference in Bali, Indonesia. The conference concluded with the adoption of the Bali Road Map, which laid out a basic direction for negotiations to reach a final agreement by 2009.

The success of this process largely depends on the participation of the two largest countries, the United States and China.

If the United States remains committed to participating in the post-Kyoto framework, there are many things that the United States and Japan can do to form consensus and to implement effective international action on this difficult but critical world issue. With regard to the fight against terrorism, the United States and Japan have already been cooperating closely. Japan strongly supported U.S. actions in Afghanistan and Iraq, and participated in both operations.

Also, the United States and Japan have already been working closely to prevent proliferation of WMD [weapons of mass destruction]. When North Korea conducted missile and nuclear tests, the United States and Japan, through action within the UN Security Council, collaborated closely in forming international joint action against North Korea and passed a resolution to impose sanctions and condemn North Korea's actions. Such cooperation was possible because Japan happened to occupy a non-permanent seat on the Security Council at the time. In this connection, I would like to draw your attention to Japan's efforts to become a permanent member of the Security Council through reforming the Council's structure and function.

Making Japan a Permanent Member

The Security Council consists of 15 members, five permanent and ten non-permanent members. The big five, the United States, United Kingdom, France, China, and Russia, have veto powers. This structure has remained unchanged since the inception of the UN, although membership has expanded from about 50 in the beginning to 192 at present, and the political power structure of the UN has drastically changed. The argument put forth by countries aspiring to become permanent members of the Security Council—namely Japan, Germany, India, and Brazil—is that there is a strong need to reform the Security Council in order to make it more reflective of today's international political realities. The specific proposal put forward by these four countries was to increase the number of seats from the present 15 to 25, including both permanent and non-permanent seats.

The United States supports Japan's bid to become a permanent member, but it does not support the others' bids and objects to expansion beyond 20 seats. The issue of Security Council reform is extremely complex as the positions of member states are so divergent. For example, Pakistan opposes India's bid to become a permanent member, China opposes Japan's bid, Argentina opposes Brazil's bid, and so on. I was deeply involved in committee discussions on this issue from 1994–97, but still today no agreement is in sight.

I believe that the key to reaching an agreement is the position of the United States, which is not thus far very enthusiastic about advancing negotiations. Japan hopes the United States will modify its position so that Japan can become a permanent member, strengthening the position of like-minded countries in the Security Council.

The UN Provides Legitimacy

At present, the United States is the largest contributor to the UN, and Japan is the second largest. How can we make the UN more effective and efficient?

First of all, I believe that the United States should recognize the utility of the UN as an invaluable instrument in advancing the interests of Western democracies as well as in tackling global issues. Most basically, the UN charter embodies the ideals espoused by the United States and other democracies. Achieving international peace and security, the respect of human rights, and the promotion of democracy are our common goals, and strong U.S. support of these principles through UN activities will immensely improve its image in the world.

From a more pragmatic viewpoint, by securing UN authorization, the United States can gain international legitimacy in its actions. A specific case in point is the decision to wage war in Iraq in 2003. When the United States sought support from allies and other countries, many countries, including Japan and the UK, urged the United States to obtain a UN Security Council resolution to specifically authorize the use of force against Saddam Hussein's regime in Iraq.

Japan and United Kingdom's argument in favor of obtaining a Security Council resolution was not strictly legal but rather political. If the UN specifically approved U.S. action, it would have been much easier politically to gain domestic support to cooperate with the United States in the war against Saddam's regime. In the end, both the UK and Japan supported U.S. action and sent forces to Iraq, but these decisions were extremely unpopular in both countries.

It is my strong belief that the United States should recognize the value of the UN, as its authorization gives legitimacy to U.S. actions, and consequently that gives allies and friendly governments more political leverage to generate domestic opinion in support of their cooperation with the United States.

In today's world, even a superpower like the United States alone cannot deal with the formidable challenges of world problems. It needs cooperation from allies and other friendly countries. Therefore, the United States must consider the political sensitiveness of other countries. Going through the UN takes time and is often a frustrating process, but it is worth trying as it would result in more effective and stronger international actions, and would ultimately better serve the interests of the United States.

Although the UN is often criticized as a huge, inefficient bureaucracy, it has accumulated and possesses tremendous expertise and knowledge in many fields, and its Secretariat has many dedicated international civil servants. We should take advantage of these assets while keeping in check the duplication and waste of international bureaucracy. The United States and Japan, as the largest and second largest donors, should work together to make the UN more efficient.

A Proper Understanding

In conclusion, I would like to make three points to summarize my presentation: First, the United Nations is neither an omnipotent nor an impotent organization. We should recognize the limits of its capabilities, but at the same time acknowledge its potential utility. It is, after all, a reflection of the realities of the international power structure. Making the UN effective and efficient requires a proper and balanced perspective on the organization. It also requires pragmatism and realism. Second, we do not have any other structure as universal as the UN, with its expertise and human resources to deal with varied global issues. We should take advantage of this asset rather than denigrating or sidelining it.

Third and lastly, there are many things that the United States and Japan can do to make the UN a more effective and efficient organization serving the best interests of our two countries and the world. In order for us to do that, proper understanding of the UN by both our peoples is indispensable.

| "In today's world, American primacy makes the UN irrelevant."

The United Nations Is Losing Its Relevancy

Joel Hainsfurther

Although the United Nations can be effective in several ways, it has largely lost its revelance, Joel Hainsfurther argues in the following viewpoint. He contends that the UN is not as relevant as it could be because the world's leaders offer no new insights when they speak at the UN. Hainsfurther further contends that another reason for the UN's loss of relevancy is the United States' primacy in foreign affairs. He acknowledges, however, that the UN remains important in areas such as peacekeeping and responding to disasters. Joel Hainsfurther is a writer and regular contributor to the Diplomatic Courier.

As you read, consider the following questions:

1. What did President George W. Bush discuss at the UN on September 23, 2008, according to the author?

2. In Hainsfurther's view, what change resulted from the September 11, 2001, terrorist attacks?

3. What does the author say that the United Nations does better than any other organization?

On September 16 [2008] the incoming President of the United Nations, Miguel d'Escoto Brockmann of Nicaragua, opened the 63rd annual Session of the UN General Assembly amidst little interest from the media about the world's biggest yearly gathering. It surprised few that Brockmann's speech discussed the importance of strengthening the power of the UN General Assembly. "The central and overarching objective of this sixty-third session of the General Assembly will be to democratize our United Nations," said Brockmann. The incoming president criticized the foreign policy of the [George W.] Bush administration, saying that no state possessed the ability to unilaterally label another state a sponsor of terrorism. He noted that this held especially true for states launching unilateral wars of aggression against nations that they regarded as state sponsors of terrorism—which he deemed the worst kind of terrorism.

One week later, on Tuesday September 23, UN Secretary-General Ban Ki-moon opened the general debate portion of the 63rd Session by remarking on the importance of global leadership and the looming economic and development crisis.

A Collection of Greatest Hits

Most of the highlights from the annual meeting occurred during the first days when the world's leaders took the floor at the General Assembly to address the international community. Their speeches contained nothing new; they were, rather, a compilation of their "greatest hits."

President Bush spoke on Tuesday September 23, stressing the importance of fighting the threats of terrorism and the proliferation of weapons of mass destruction by rogue regimes. "The nations of this body must stand united in the fight against terror. We must continue working to deny the terrorists refuge anywhere in the world, including ungoverned spaces. We must remain vigilant against proliferation—by fully implementing the terms of Security Council Resolution 1540 [requiring member states to take action against the proliferation of weapons of mass destruction], and enforcing sanctions against North Korea and Iran. We must not relent until out people are safe from this threat to civilization," declared Bush.

Later that afternoon, President Mahmoud Ahmadinejad of the Islamic Republic of Iran accosted the General Assembly. Ahmadinejad declared that the "American empire in the world is reaching the end of its road, and its next rulers must limit their interference to their own borders. Today, the thought of hegemony quickly becomes a demerit." He added that the "Zionist regime is on a definite slope to collapse." Ahmadinejad reaffirmed the position of Iran that its nuclear program exists solely for peaceful civilian purposes.

French President Nicolas Sarkozy announced that France respects Iran's right to maintain a peaceful nuclear energy program but that it would not approve of a nuclear-armed Iran or a regime that threatens the demise of the state of Israel.

The following morning President Hamid Karzai of Afghanistan discussed the importance of continuing to combat terrorism. "Undoubtedly, terrorism will not go away until we dismantle the elaborate institutional support terrorists enjoy in the region and eliminate their secure sanctuaries." That afternoon, President Demetris Christofias of the Republic of Cyprus addressed the assembly about the ongoing efforts to negotiate a peace agreement with the Turkish-Cypriots in order to unite the island of Cyprus.

On Thursday morning President Jalal Talabani of Iraq spoke about security issues in his country and called on all nations to increase their diplomatic presence in Iraq. On Saturday afternoon, Mr. Pak Kil Yon—the Vice Minister for foreign affairs of the Democratic Peoples Republic of Korea (DPRK)—accused the United States of being the worst perpetrator of human rights violations in the world. He also asserted that the United States' insistence on unilateral inspections of North Korea's nuclear facilities amounted to an attempt to violate the country's sovereignty.

Do People Care About the UN?

And so it went; the major players all spoke. Yet, all of this begs the question; does anybody care about what they said? If anybody read the news last week, they would be led to believe that the answer is no. The 63rd Session of the General Assembly received relatively little news coverage, and most people probably do not even know that the UN General Assembly was in session. Instead, Americans and others around the world turned their attention towards the first presidential debate and Congress' attempt to save the financial industry and the economy. Would attention still be diverted, however, if those stories were not the news of the day or do people simply not care about the UN anymore?

In the past several years the United Nations has experienced a sort of an identity crisis. Amidst scandals such as oil for food and sexual misconduct perpetrated by UN Peacekeepers, the world's organization increasingly struggles with growing criticism.

The UN's critics call the organization an irrelevant institution that fails to accomplish anything meaningful; they call it out of date, and believe that it serves a world that no longer exists.

When the UN was established 63 years ago, it reflected the realities of a world shattered by WWII [World War II]. The post–Cold War unipolar world order differs greatly from the political environment that existed after WWII. The terrorist attacks on September 11 brought about a fundamental change in the nature of American primacy; acting as the world's hegemonic power, the United States relied on unilateralism, military force, and preventive war instead of traditional diplomatic tools in its efforts to reshape the world according to its vision.

America Makes the UN Irrelevant

After WWII, the "winners" established the UN and used it to rebuild the Axis Powers into liberal democratic allies. Through this forum these allies worked together to contain the communist ideology of the Soviets and other communist regimes. In today's world, American primacy makes the UN irrelevant. A growing ideological divide between western liberal democracies and authoritarian regimes further undermines the organization's ability to make any substantive progress in regards to pressing international issues. With 192 nations represented at the UN—many of them being a part of other alliances and all looking out for their own national interests—reaching a consensus seems impossible.

The world today is not the world of 1945 and the institutions of 1945 do not reflect the state of the world today. Nowhere is that better reflected than in the most coveted UN Security Council [UNSC]. Five nations—the United States, France, the United Kingdom, Russia, and China—sit permanently on the UNSC and have the power to veto any resolution that comes to a vote. Other members can take turns occupying the additional ten rotating seats on the UNSC. While many member nations have sought to reform the Security Council, they have failed to establish a consensus about how to reform it.

The UNSC, which more often than not finds itself deeply paralyzed and divided across ideological lines, cannot reach a consensus on the majority of the issues. If the UNSC usually fails to find a consensus, it is even more difficult for the General Assembly to establish a consensus and act on important issues such as human rights and nuclear disarmament. When the UNSC does pass a resolution, it is difficult to ensure that it is fully enforced.

The UN Can Be Effective

While the UN appears irrelevant when it comes to solving global security and economic issues, the organization remains extremely effective in several important areas. The UN arguably coordinates relief efforts for natural disasters better than any other organization in the world. The UN also does a good job of promoting cultural and educational exchange and it is the one place the world turns to when major humanitarian or natural disasters occur. The organization's peacekeeping missions are often preferable to violent and expensive wars and ultimately lead to favorable outcomes.

The organization has made a genuine effort the past five years to reform and bounce back from multiple scandals. During the oil for food program, [Iraqi dictator] Saddam's regime earned up to $11 billion despite being under UN sanctions. Corruption within the UN, as well as poor oversight from the UNSC is what allowed for such a scandal to thrive. At a UN summit in 2005 [UN secretary-general Kofi] Annan introduced reforms aimed at increasing oversight and accountability and also at reforming ethics. Many of those reforms have already taken place and others are still on the way.

The debate on the relevancy of the UN is not a new one and cannot be bundled into the "Multilateralism vs. Unilateralism" argument. While the UN has failed in its mission to resolve international security issues, it succeeded wildly in humanitarian responses, aid distribution, and preserving world heritage sites. Ultimately, the UN is only as good as its members; they will determine the future relevancy of the organization.

| *"The United Nations has a competitive edge in political facilitation and humanitarian assistance."*

The United Nations Has Many Goals Still to Achieve

Ban Ki-moon, interviewed by Ray Suarez

In the following viewpoint, UN Secretary-General Ban Ki-moon details to reporter Ray Suarez several of the goals that the United Nations hopes to achieve. According to Ban, these goals include responding to the humanitarian crises in Myanmar and Darfur, addressing the problem of global warming, and contributing to peace and security in Iraq. In these and other instances, Ban asserts, the UN needs cooperation from the worldwide community. Suarez is a senior correspondent for PBS Newshour.

As you read, consider the following questions:

1. Why is it necessary for factional rebel groups to participate in political negotiations to solve the crisis in Darfur, according to Ban?

2. What is the secretary-general's first action plan for Darfur?

Ray Suarez, "Transcript: U.N. Chief Forging New Solutions on Climate, Conflicts: Interview with Ban Ki-moon," *PBS Newshour*, October 11, 2007. Copyright © 2007 MacNeil/Lehrer Productions. Reproduced by permission.

3. According to Ban, what three ideas does the UN plan to promote in Iraq?

*R*AY SUAREZ: *I spoke with Secretary-General Ban Ki-moon before he started a round of meetings today in Washington. Secretary-General Ban, welcome to the program.*
BAN KI-MOON: It's a great pleasure to meet you.

The UN in Myanmar and Darfur

Does the United Nations have any leverage in Myanmar? Can it really stay the hand of a government that means to suppress the democracy movement?

The United Nations itself has the highest moral voice, as far as principled methods of democracy and human rights are concerned, and we have been mobilizing all possible political influences of leaders in the region and in the world.

I have spoken with many leaders in ASEAN [Association of Southeast Asian Nations], and ASEAN recently has taken a very strong position vis-a-vis Myanmar's human rights situation. We have put forward some proposals demanding the release of political detainees, and make socioeconomic and political democratizations. These efforts will be continuously done at the level of myself and through my special envoy.

You've just recently returned from Darfur. You spoke to people in the camps, spoke to people in the government of Sudan. Where do things stand now?

Now we are looking forward to the political negotiations, which will be held on October 27th [2007]. Necessary preparations are going on at the final phase.

What we are now working hard [on] is to have all the rebel group leaders participate in these political preparations, political negotiations. We hope that they should demonstrate their commitment as leaders of all these rebel movements, if they think about the future of their country that they must participate, rather than staying out of these political negotiations.

Now, the deployment of a joint hybrid operation in Darfur is also going on smoothly.

Three Plans for Darfur

The government in Khartoum has said all along that not enough attention has been paid to the rebel groups that are fighting against the central government that Sudan says is the real cause for the humanitarian crisis. Does the rebel movement, these various armies, have to be part of the peace process in order for the dying and the killing to stop there?

It is necessary for those factional groups to participate in these political negotiations because they are the important stakeholders. We will have political negotiations where their concerns could be heard.

And the continuing violence will gain nothing. They must cease these violent means, and there should be a cessation of hostilities immediately. Sudan's government has assured that, as soon as these political negotiations begin, they will declare a unilateral cessation of the hostilities. I do hope that all of the rebel groups will participate in this cessation of hostilities.

Now, another big world problem facing the U.N. that you've spoken out about is global warming, but in your view, global warming is part of the Darfur crisis, as well. Tell us about that.

The Darfur crisis, in fact, was a man-made crisis, but you cannot rule out all these aspects of environmental degradation, the absolute poverty, as well as the scarcity of natural resources, particularly water. That has exacerbated all these situations.

Therefore, we must take some comprehensive resolution of this Darfur situation. This is what I have been doing. I have three action plans.

One is ensuring peace and security in Darfur. Then, resolve this issue through political negotiations. Without a political negotiation, you cannot ensure a smooth peace and security there. Then, there should be some hope, sign of hope to the Darfurian people through developmental packages.

Therefore, my plan is to have all this comprehensive addressing in three tracks. They are now moving, and we have made some credible progresses. But the important thing will have to come from now until we see the final resolution of this issue.

Global Warming and Iraq

But if there's no worldwide approach toward greenhouse gases and global climate change, will there be more Darfurs in the world?

I am very much encouraged by the level of strong support from the world in recognizing the urgency of this global warming situation. The science has made it quite clear, and we have been feeling the impact coming from global warming.

If we do not take actions, you cannot guarantee that we will not see any second Darfurian situations there. I will continuously be engaged, but we need strong support. This is a global challenge which requires a global response, common and concerted efforts.

But let's take a look at the permanent five [P-5] in the Security Council. Sitting on the permanent five are two of the world's biggest polluters—China and the United States—a major oil exporter—Russia—and two very carbon-intense societies in Britain and France. Are these the five countries that are really going to help get the world to agree to emit fewer greenhouse gases?

It's true that each and every country, not necessarily the P-5, but all the countries, they have their own domestic challenges. But what is encouraging is that all the countries now recognize the significance and urgency and importance of taking common action to address these global warming issues.

I am encouraged that the United States has also confirmed that the United Nations should take the leading role, and the United States is also very much committed to this process.

The United Nations hasn't had a large-scale presence in Iraq since the attack on the U.N. compound there. It's been some time since then. And now the American political leadership and the candidates to take over the presidency are talking about having fewer American troops there over time. Will this create an opening for the reengagement of the world community in Iraq, the reengagement of the U.N.?

As the secretary-general, I am in the process of very seriously considering how the United Nations can increase our presence there, how we can make a different contribution to peace and security there.

However, the United Nations does not have all the necessary resources or tools. Our security and safety has been largely dependent upon the MNF [Multi-National Force] forces. However, we've been taking necessary, again, preparations to have integrated security accommodations for our staff and our activities there.

We are going to help promote national reconciliation, a national dialogue, and help promote regional cooperation. The United Nations has a competitive edge in political facilitation and humanitarian assistance. This is what we are now considering.

But you also have to have a welcome from the United States and from the government of Iraq to be involved there. Do you have that now?

As the situation develops in the future, I know that the United Nations will have to be engaged more, and the United Nations needs full cooperation and support from all of the international community, including the United States and other big powers, and particularly the Iraqi government.

Encouraging Signs in North Korea

Recently, there was a meeting between the heads of state of the two Koreas. Was this an encouraging sign? Do you think it actually helps build down the tension on the [Korean] peninsula?

I am very much encouraged as secretary-general of the United Nations, as one of the Korean citizens, to have seen this very moving development of situation. It will certainly pave the way to solidify the common ground.

And stop the North Korean nuclear program?

North Korea has committed to disenable their nuclear facilities, with the ultimate proposal for dismantling all nuclear weapons and nuclear programs. This is, again, a very good, encouraging sign toward the denuclearization of the Korean peninsula.

This will, again, bring the peace and security not only on the Korean peninsula, but beyond this Korean peninsula in Northeast Asia.

Ban Ki-moon, Mr. Secretary-General, thanks a lot.

It gives me great pleasure. Thank you.

Periodical Bibliography

The following articles have been selected to supplement the diverse views presented in this chapter.

Morton Abramowitz and Thomas Pickering — "Making Intervention Work: Improving the UN's Ability to Act," *Foreign Affairs*, September-October 2008.

Mark Malloch Brown — "The John W. Holmes Lecture: Can the UN Be Reformed?" *Global Governance*, January-March, 2008.

Jonah Goldberg — "Justice League," *National Review*, August 27, 2007.

Charles A. Kupchan — "Minor League, Major Problems," *Foreign Affairs*, November-December 2008.

Celestino Migliore — "Hopes for U.N. Reform: The Serious Disorder in World Affairs Requires a Global Remedy," *America*, June 20, 2005.

Sally Morphet — "Future Prospects for the United Nations," *Global Governance*, January-March, 2007.

Justin Raimondo — "Gang of Democracies," *American Conservative*, October 6, 2008.

Greg Reeson — "Has the UN Become Irrelevant?" *American Chronicle*, August 10, 2006.

Michael Soussan — "Can the UN Be Fixed?" *Commentary*, April 2005.

Shashi Tharoor — "What the United Nations Needs," *Newsweek International*, September 4, 2006.

C. Eduardo Vargas Toro — "UN Security Council Reform: Unrealistic Proposals and Viable Reform Options," *American Diplomacy*, November 25, 2008.

For Further Discussion

Chapter 1

1. After reading the selections in this chapter, do you believe the United Nations is an effective organization? Why or why not?

2. One theme in this chapter is criticism of the UN's Human Rights Council. After reading the relevant viewpoints, do you feel the council needs to be reformed? If so, what steps would you suggest?

3. Asha-Rose Migiro and Richard Williamson have both worked at the UN. How does this impact your reading of their viewpoints?

Chapter 2

1. UN Watch and the U.S. Department of State disagree on whether the United Nations is anti-Israel. Whose argument do you find more convincing, and why?

2. Do you agree with Maya Rosenfeld's conclusion that the UNRWA does not support terrorism? If so, which part of her argument do you find most convincing? If not, what do you feel is lacking in her argument?

3. After reading the viewpoints in this chapter, what do you think would be the best way for the United Nations to ensure that all nations in the Middle East are treated fairly?

Chapter 3

1. John F. McManus believes that the United States should leave the United Nations. If that were to happen, what do you think would be the impact on the UN?

2. Brett Schaefer and Steven Groves contend that the United States must push for reforms at the UN. Based on the readings in this and the other chapters, how do you think other nations would respond to a U.S.-led reform movement? Explain your answer.

3. After reading the viewpoints by Susan Rice and Meryl Frank, do you support or disapprove of the Obama administration's approach to the UN? Explain your answer.

Chapter 4

1. After reading the viewpoints in this chapter, do you believe the UN will be a relevant organization in twenty years? Why or why not?

2. Rodrigue Tremblay asserts that the UN Security Council needs to be reformed, while Sven Bernhard Gareis and Johannes Varwick contend that such reforms are unlikely. Whose argument do you find more convincing and why?

3. In his interview, Ban Ki-moon details several goals for the UN. Which of these goals do you believe is most likely to be achieved? Which is least likely? Explain your answers.

Organizations to Contact

American Policy Center
70 Main Street, Suite 23, Warrenton, VA   20186
(540) 341-8911 • fax: (540) 341-8917
e-mail: ampolicycenter@hotmail.com
Web site: www.americanpolicy.org

The American Policy Center is a nonprofit foundation dedicated to promoting free enterprise and limited government. Among the issues that it focuses on is the United Nations and how it impacts American sovereignty. Articles critical of the UN are available on its Web site. In addition, the center publishes the *DeWeese Report* and the *Insider's Report*.

The Heritage Foundation
214 Massachusetts Ave. NE, Washington, DC   20002-4999
(202) 546-4400
e-mail: info@heritage.org
Web site: www.heritage.org

The Heritage Foundation seeks to promote conservative public policies based on principles such as limited government and a strong national defense. The foundation also believes that the United States needs to create alternatives to the UN. Foundation members have provided testimony and written papers in Heritage's Backgrounder series on the United Nations, including *Elections for U.N. Human Rights Council Underscore the Need for Reform* and *Time to Rein in the U.N.'s Budget*.

Human Rights Watch (HRW)
350 Fifth Ave., 34th Floor, New York, NY   10018-3299
(212) 290-4700 • fax: (212) 736-1300
Web site: www.hrw.org

Human Rights Watch is an independent organization that aims to protect and defend human rights. HRW has a section on its Web site devoted to the UN, with reports including *"There Is No Protection": Insecurity and Human Rights in Southern Sudan.*

United Nations Association of the United States of America (UNA-USA)
801 Second Ave., 2nd Floor, New York, NY   10017-4706
(212) 907-1300 • fax: (212) 682-9185
e-mail: unahq@unausa.org
Web site: www.unausa.org

UNA-USA is an organization that seeks to educate American people about the important work of the United Nations. The association also promotes the need for the United States to be a constructive leader at the UN. UNA-USA produces a variety of publications, including the magazine *InterDependent*, the e-newsletter *UNA-USA World Bulletin*, factsheets, and papers.

United Nations Children's Fund (UNICEF)
UNICEF House, 3 United Nations Plaza, New York, NY   10017
(212) 326-7000 • fax: (212) 887-7465
Web site: www.unicef.org

The purpose of UNICEF is to help children around the world overcome poverty, disease, and violence. The organization believes that providing care for children from a very young age helps ensure a strong future. Resources on its Web site include press releases and factsheets.

United Nations Educational, Scientific, and Cultural Organization (UNESCO)
7 place de Fontenoy 75352, Paris   07 SP
   France
+33 1 45 68 10 00 • fax: +33 1 45 67 16 90
Web site: www.unesco.org

The goal of UNESCO is to improve dialogue among different civilizations and cultures, based on respect for common values. Through this dialogue, UNESCO aims to improve human rights and alleviate poverty. Factsheets are available on its Web site.

United Nations Foundation

1800 Massachusetts Ave. NW, Suite 400
Washington, DC   20036
(202) 887-9040 • fax: (202) 887-9021
Web site: www.unfoundation.org

The UN Foundation is a public charity that advocates for the UN and supports UN activities. The foundation also serves as a platform to connect people and ideas in order to assist the UN in solving global problems. Press releases, fact sheets, and publications can be found on its Web site, including *Start with a Girl: A New Agenda for Global Health*.

United Nations High Commission for Refugees (UNHCR)

Case Postale 2500, Genève 2 Dépôt   CH-1211
   Switzerland
+41 22 739 8111
Web site: www.unhcr.org

The UNHCR seeks to protect refugees and help them restart their lives, including finding safe refuge or resettling in another country. The agency has a staff of more than sixty-six hundred people in over 110 countries. Its publications include annual global reports; statistics and news are also among the resources on its Web site.

United States Mission to the United Nations (USUN)

Press and Public Diplomacy Section, New York, NY   10017
(212) 415-4062 • fax: (212) 415-4053
Web site: www.usunnewyork.usmission.gov

The U.S. Mission to the United Nations is the United States' delegation to the United Nations. Fact sheets, press releases, and speeches can be found on its Web site. In addition, information on issues such as UN reform and climate change is also available on the site.

UN Watch

Case Postale 191, Geneva 20   1211
  Switzerland
+41 22 734 1472 • fax: +41 22 734 1613
Web site: www.unwatch.org

UN Watch is a nongovernmental organization whose mission is to make sure that the UN treats all of its member states equally. In particular, the organization provides information on the disproportionate attention given to Israel. News, stories, testimony, articles, and reports are available on its Web site, including the reports *Mutual Praise Society* and *Evaluation of 2010–2013 UN Human Rights Council Candidates.*

Bibliography of Books

Francis Adams
The United Nations in Latin America: Aiding Development. New York: Routledge, 2010.

Peter R. Baehr and Leon Gordenker
The United Nations: Reality and Ideal. New York: Palgrave Macmillan, 2006.

John Bolton
Surrender Is Not an Option: Defending America at the United Nations. New York: Threshold Editions, 2007.

David L. Bosco
Five to Rule Them All: The UN Security Council and the Making of the Modern World. New York: Oxford University Press, 2009.

Kevin P. Clements and Nadia Mizner, eds.
The Center Holds: UN Reform for 21st Century Challenges. New Brunswick, NJ: Transaction, 2008.

Victor D. Comras
Flawed Diplomacy: The United Nations and the War on Terrorism. Dulles, VA: Potomac Books, 2010.

Michael W. Doyle and Nicholas Sambanis
Making War and Building Peace: United Nations Peace Operations. Princeton, NJ: Princeton University Press, 2006.

Linda Fasulo
An Insider's Guide to the UN. New Haven, CT: Yale University Press, 2009.

Sven Bernhard Gareis and Johannes Varwick — *The United Nations: An Introduction.* New York: Palgrave Macmillan, 2005.

Dore Gold — *Tower of Babble: How the United Nations Has Fueled Global Chaos.* New York: Three Rivers, 2005.

Richard Jolly, Louis Emmerij, and Thomas G. Weiss — *UN Ideas That Changed the World.* Bloomington: Indiana University Press, 2009.

Paul Kennedy — *The Parliament of Man: The Past, Present, and Future of the United Nations.* New York: Vintage Books, 2007.

Jeane J. Kirkpatrick — *Making War to Keep Peace.* New York: HarperCollins, 2007.

Adam LeBor — *"Complicity with Evil": The United Nations in the Age of Modern Genocide.* New Haven, CT: Yale University Press, 2006.

Mark Mazower — *No Enchanted Palace: The End of Empire and the Ideological Origins of the United Nations.* Princeton, NJ: Princeton University Press, 2009.

Stanley Meisler — *Kofi Annan: A Man of Peace in a World of War.* Hoboken, NJ: Wiley, 2007.

Julie A. Mertus — *The United Nations and Human Rights: A Guide for a New Era.* New York: Routledge, 2009.

Karen A. Mingst and Margaret P. Karns — *The United Nations in the Twenty-first Century*. Boulder, CO: Westview, 2006.

Roger Normand and Sarah Zaidi — *Human Rights at the UN: The Political History of Universal Justice*. Bloomington: Indiana University Press, 2007.

Samantha Power — *Chasing the Flame: Sergio Vieria de Mello and the Fight to Save the World*. New York: Penguin, 2008.

Eric Shawn — *The U.N. Exposed: How the United Nations Sabotages America's Security and Fails the World*. New York: Sentinel Trade, 2006.

Andrzej Sitkowski — *UN Peacekeeping: Myth and Reality*. Westport, CT: Praeger Security International, 2006.

James Traub — *The Best Intentions: Kofi Annan and the UN in the Era of American World Power*. New York: Farrar, Straus & Giroux, 2006.

Thomas G. Weiss — *What's Wrong with the United Nations and How to Fix It*. Cambridge: Polity, 2008.

Spencer Zifcak — *United Nations Reform: Heading North or South?* New York: Routledge, 2009.

Index